Homosexuality

In the 21st Century

by Alan Philowitz

©2014

Table of Contents

Introduction

The development of individuals' sexuality is complex and not completely understood. Homosexuality is a form of sexual expression that is as complex as heterosexuality. Homosexual acts have been recorded in thousands of species of animals, and it is clear that homosexuality has a place in the spectrum of behaviors performed by humans. Homosexuality is controversial for all individuals, including homosexuals, because it is not a dominant sexual orientation. Despite homosexuality not being entirely understood by many individuals in society and scientists, it will be continued to be practiced whether it is sanctioned or not. Homosexuality is part of human history, and it is clear that it has been practiced in conjunction with heterosexuality by human beings for millennia. One of the major issues facing homosexuals within society is heterosexuals' lack of understanding of same-sex practices, and the shared commonalities that homosexuality has with heterosexuality. Whether individuals within a society agree with the practice of homosexuality or not, central to the acceptance of homosexual practices is the right to sexual freedom. Regardless of the genetic or environmental influences that contribute to people's sexual orientation, individuals should have the legal right in practice homosexuality with other consenting individuals in adulthood.

In the twenty-first century, the Gay Rights Movement has continued to lobby and expose the victimization and discriminations of homosexuals throughout the world. Despite homosexuals still being victimized and punished by death in countries throughout the world, it is clear that some progress has been made toward the acceptance of homosexual practices as a result of the

Gay Rights Movement, especially in Western countries. The central issue throughout the world in relation to the acceptance of homosexuality is not same-sex orientation itself but sexual freedom. Countries that continue to permit victimization of individuals persecute individuals legally based on sexual orientation are not against homosexuals but are opposed to sexual freedom. In modern secular societies, there should be no government restrictions on individuals' sexual freedom, and individuals should be able to practice any and all consenting sexual acts that they wish.

Homosexuality and other non-heterosexual acts, however, are not mainstream, so their level of acceptance in society will never be as great as heterosexuality. Homosexual acts are as natural as heterosexual acts, but they do not lead to descendants without the help of science. Homosexuals should not be forced into heterosexual relationships and lifestyles, and there should be an underlying recognition by the homosexual community that heterosexuality is necessary for all functioning societies because of the need to continually reproduce members to sustain growth. This is necessary for many reasons, but societies must add new members from births to avoid decline. Homosexuals do have a place within society, and they do have a right to have their sexual freedom respected by others and enforced through legislation.

Two popular issues regarding homosexual rights in Western societies today are same-sex marriage and same-sex adoption. The issues are both complex and different at their core, but they are similar in that the Gay Right Movement has brought two huge issues to the forefront of politics, which exposes major differences in the legal rights between heterosexual and homosexual couples within varying societies and legal systems. The issue of marriage has been made unnecessarily complex by incorporating religious arguments into it, and it is clear that this is a result of marriages being historically sanctioned and blessed by religious institutions. Under modern secular governments, homosexuals should be permitted to be legally wed in common law marriages and afforded all the rights that common law marriages give to heterosexual couples. Homosexuality is a sin, and it should not be practiced by religious individuals. Religious institutions should not sanction or bless homosexual marriages in accordance with their theological texts, interpretations, and sanctioned practices. Religious institutions in the modern era have increasingly been preaching abstinence of homosexual practices but accepting individuals with same-sex orientations into their communities. This is clearly contradictory to religious institutions historical practices and the nature of individuals as sexual beings, and these policies are not only confusing but results in practices unnecessarily problematic for religious communities' members and homosexuals alike. Homosexuals and homosexuality should be tolerated by religious institutions in accordance with the laws in countries in which they reside, but searching scientific answers regarding the origins of homosexuality to increase acceptance of members who are homosexual in the modern era is pointless because it contradicts religious institutions theological texts, teachings, and historical practices. It also confuses heterosexual members regarding spiritual teachings and can potentially harm homosexuals psychologically by making them conform to heterosexual ideals.

Same-sex adoption is more complex than homosexual marriage from a legal perspective because the issue is not only centered on potential rights for parents but rights of children. Homosexuals are presently able to adopt children in most states across the United States. It is clear that this decision was made based more on a need for adoptive parents and needs of adoptive parents than on research on homosexual parental practices and their outcomes. Presently, nearly 5% of the children adopted in the US are done so by homosexual couples, and the research that has been performed suggests that children adopted by gay and lesbian couples have similar behavior performance to those adopted by heterosexual couples (Adoptive Families Magazine, 2014). Florida is currently the only state that bans homosexual couples from adopting, but most states still have legal barriers in place for same-sex couples, which results in only a single member of same-sex couples being legally able to adopt. The trend of homosexual couples adopting will continue well into the future despite the lack of regard for a child's right to a mother and father. The fact that adopted children are being put in the care of same-sex couples that cannot biologically reproduce on their own may benefit them in a novel manner because they are actually wanted. It is clear that same-sex couples may not offer a traditional family scenario to adopted children, but they do offer a loving solution to children who have not been provided it in the past and are not likely to receive it at transition facilities in between homes. It is clear that social services in the US has made the right decision regarding placing children in need in loving homes with individuals who want to care for them, but it is not clear if the psychological benefits of placing children in loving homes outweighs the potential psychological harm of placing children in the care of non-traditional parents.

It is clear that the Gay Rights Movement will not subside as societies progress further into the twenty-first century. The next frontier for those seeking sexual freedom will be in non-Western countries that still permit victimization and death based on same-sex preference in their societies. The Gay Rights Movement must maintain gains that it has made permitting its sexual freedom in Western countries, and continue to function as an accepted entity within predominantly heterosexual societies were their right to be accepted as members of society is legally established. It is clear that homosexuals still face issues surrounding discrimination and marginalization even in societies that have legislation protecting them, which directly impacts all aspects of their lives. Heterosexuals have an obligation to recognize that homosexuality is part of human behavior that has been practiced at varying degrees throughout our history. Whether an individual agrees with homosexuality or not, a person has a right to sexual freedom, and this should be respected in a civilized manner that is reflective of the modern secular legislation that permits it. Heterosexism and homophobia often exhibit themselves in similar ways, but they both result from a lack of understanding and knowledge toward homosexuality and the human experience. Despite some heterosexuals' lack of understanding of homosexuality, they must accept it, and work to create societies that are accepting of individuals sexual preferences and that respect sexual freedom.

Chapter 1: Homosexuality

Homosexuality is an interest and attraction to one's own sex (homosexuality, 2014). Homosexuals are often referred to as gays, and homosexual females are often referred to as lesbians. Homosexuality has been accepted, punished, and banned at various times throughout history in societies throughout the world. Homosexuality was common in ancient Greece and Rome in which homosexual relationships between adult men and adolescent males were widely accepted. Jewish, Christian, and Muslim cultures have typically perceived and instructed their followers that homosexuality was sinful, specifically the acts of homosexuality and not the individual homosexuals. There has been a shift within these faiths, both theologically and socially, to fully accept homosexuals and their relationships, which has caused separations in denominations throughout the world.

Beliefs toward homosexuality in modern times have continued to shift as a result of political activism by homosexuals within society, and within most societies views toward homosexuality range from complete acceptance to homosexual acts being considered to be psychologically deviant (homosexuality, 2014). The American Psychological Association removed ego-syntonic homosexuality or the mental condition of one accepting their homosexuality from the "Diagnostic and Statistical Manual of Mental Disorders" in 1973. There are religious groups throughout the world that continue to emphasize abstinence for homosexuals and curing homosexuality through prayer, counseling, and behavior modification.

From the beginning of the nineteenth century until the end of the twentieth century psychologists classified homosexuality as a form of mental illness, and there were numerous theories developed regarding its origin (homosexuality, 2014). Richard von Krafft-Ebing classified homosexuality in "Psychopathia Sexualis" in 1886 in a list of perversions that he believed originated from genetics. During the same period, Sigmund Freud believed that homosexuality resulted from a psychosexual conflict in the development of individuals resulting from identification with the parent of the opposite sex. Other psychologists during this period investigated social influences and physiological developments as potential origins of the development of homosexuality, but it is now believed that homosexuality, like all behavior, results from a combination of genetics and environment.

At the end of the twentieth century and the beginning of the twenty-first century, many Western societies increased in their acceptance of homosexuality, and it is now accepted as a common expression of human sexuality (homosexuality, 2014). Many of the stereotypes classifying male homosexuals as being weak and feminine and lesbians as being aggressive and masculine have been discarded. The growing acceptance of homosexuality as a common expression of human sexuality was partially a result of research performed through the second half of the twentieth century. Alfred Kinsey conducted social and behavioral science experiments in the United States in the 1950s, which found that homosexual activity was a frequent expression of human sexuality found in both adolescent males and females. Kinsey found the about 30% of adult males and 15% of females had engaged in some form of homosexual activity, and he observed a spectrum of sexual activity that was influenced by situational activity in which opportunities for heterosexual contact was shown to be a factor.

Societies throughout the world respond different to homosexual activity, and homosexual activity and behavior is considered unacceptable in countries throughout Latin America, Asia, and Africa (homosexuality, 2014). Western countries have been considered to be historically more liberal, but it was considered unacceptable to discuss the topic of homosexuality throughout the nineteenth century and most of the twentieth century in public forums. Homosexuality became a political movement in the United States at the end of the twentieth century with the Gay Rights Movement. Following the political movement, many homosexuals began to identify themselves as gay or lesbian to their friends, families, and the public. Many homosexuals began to demand equal rights in employment practices, housing, and public policies during this period. For the majority of the population in North America and Europe, this marked an initial awareness of homosexual communities for the first time. As a response to the political activism, jurisdictions throughout Western countries began to enact legislation that banned discrimination against homosexuals, and employers in these regions began to offer domestic partner benefits for healthcare benefits and insurance coverage.

Conditions for homosexuals have continued to improve in Western countries throughout the twenty-first century, but violence toward homosexuals has continued in many parts of the world (homosexuality, 2014). Homosexuals continue to be routinely beaten throughout Central and South America, and they are still not legally protected against violence throughout most parts of Africa. Many anti-homosexual groups within these regions have been responsible for murdering homosexuals and continue to threaten gay rights groups with violence. Intolerance toward homosexuals is accepted in most non-Western countries, and many analysts believe that this has persisted into the twenty-first century directly as a result of religion and acquired immunodeficiency syndrome. AIDS has been a serious issue worldwide for over three decades, but in many Western countries the virus was particularly widespread through homosexual communities. As a result of this, homosexuals were on the forefront in advocating research into AIDS and support for the victims of the disease. Fear of the disease and the media coverage that followed has contributed to the negative treatment of homosexuals despite the majority of AIDS transmissions outside of Western countries resulting mostly throughout heterosexual sex.

Medicine and Homosexuality

The removal of homosexuality from the "Diagnostic and Statistical Manual of Mental Disorders" by the American Psychiatric Association almost entirely as a behavioral disorder in 1980 showed a dramatic reversal in perceptions regarding homosexuality (Friedman & Downey, 1994). In psychiatric medicine, it is important to differentiate between normal and abnormal behaviors, so treatment offered can be effective and follow contemporary standards. The present state of knowledge regarding homosexuality is important in understanding historical perspectives of the behavior, and it is central to understanding the sexual orientation and psychological functioning of homosexuals within society.

The term homosexual became commonly used in Europe in the late nineteenth century, and the term gay in reference to homosexuals became popular in the 1970s with the Gay Rights Movement (Friedman & Downey, 1994). In replications of Kinsey's study on homosexual behavior in the 70s and 80s with a more general sample population, it was shown that his findings regarding the level of homosexual behavior in society were nearly correct. The data on individuals admitting exclusive homosexual contact is about 2% of the adult male population, and the data on the current prevalence of exclusive female homosexuality is considered insufficient. Homosexuality has been historically underreported as a result of social prejudice, and it is believed that many female homosexuals are included in populations of heterosexuals in research regarding populations' sexual orientation as a result of this discrimination. It is also believed that many female homosexuals engage in heterosexual intercourse without arousal, and most studies do not include sexual fantasies about the same-sex in measurements of individuals' sexual orientations.

Regardless of individuals' sexual orientation, 75% of American youth have had sexual relations with another individual by the age of 18 (Friedman & Downey, 1994). Homosexual males are more likely than heterosexual males to become sexually active at an earlier age, and they are more likely than heterosexual males to have had multiple sexual partners. For homosexual and heterosexual females, the age at the time of one's first sexual experience is closer. Of the general population of heterosexual men that are sexually active, 20% have had one sex partner, 55% have had up 20 partners, and 25% have had 20 or more partners over the course of their lives. Of populations of homosexual men that are sexually active, most have had 20 or fewer sexual partners during their lives, and less than 1% of homosexual men have had 100 or more partners. Despite women being studied less than men, the data that has been collected shows that heterosexual and homosexual women resemble each other, and this is believed by researchers to result from women attributing sexual desires as a function of emotional intimacy and increases value on monogamy. Research shows that nearly all heterosexual women who are married and sexually active are unlikely to have more than one partner, and although homosexual female couples have less sexual activity than heterosexual couples they have fewer partners outside their relationships and report increased satisfaction within their relationships.

A minority of the adult population remains abstinent from sexual activity in the United States on an annual basis (Friedman & Downey, 1994). Of homosexual men, 12% remain abstinent annually, and 43% of lesbians remain abstinent for a year or more. Of the sexually active adult population in the US, diverse sexual practices occur in various groups regardless of sexual orientation. Studies suggest that over 75% of both heterosexuals and homosexuals engage in oral sex, but homosexuals have reported doing so more frequently. Anal sex is practiced by both heterosexual and homosexual couples, but the practice is six times more frequent between homosexual couples. Homosexual men are considered to be at a high risk for human immunodeficiency virus because of the potential of contact with semen during unprotected receptive anal intercourse, and other sexual practices that attribute to an exchange of body fluids. In the last three decades, efforts to educate and change the practices of homosexual men have been partially effective, and research has shown that homosexual men who typically engage in unprotected anal intercourse with multiple partners are young, minorities, engage in acts frequently, use drugs or alcohol, and have mental disorders. These men are believed to entertain false notions regarding their potential level of safety in contracting HIV, and 45% of sexually active homosexual men report having lapses in safe sex practices.

Homosexual females who have been found to be HIV-positive nearly always contract the disease as a result of exposure to other risk factors rather than contact with a partner (Friedman & Downey, 1994). Vaginal secretions and menstrual blood are known to cause transmission of HIV, so homosexual females in relationships with HIV-positive partners or who have multiple partners are encouraged to use safe sex practices. Unfortunately, there has been no adequate medically tested strategy developed for homosexual females to avoid contact with partners' bodily fluids that properly addresses issues presented by female anatomy and physiology. In general, homosexual males have a higher risk for sexually transmitted diseases in comparison to the general population of sexually active adults.

Chapter 2: Homophobia

The term homophobia began to be used in the 1960s to signify irrational negative attitudes toward homosexuals within society, and in Western societies the two prominent influences of homophobia have been religious fundamentalism and heterosexism (Friedman & Downey, 1994). There has been a widespread tendency throughout history to view homosexuality as disgraceful and to humiliate homosexual people, but this has begun to lessen in the last four decades in Western countries. Studies have indicated that homophobic people are authoritarian, conservative, and religious. They typically live in regions in which negative attitudes toward homosexual people are viewed as normal, and they have not generally had a great deal of personal contact with any homosexual people. Many of the negative views of homosexual individuals are similar to other prejudices seen within society. Most homosexual individuals have been harassed or threatened at some point during their lives as a result of their sexual orientation. Homophobia differs from other prejudices within society because many homosexual individuals grow up passing themselves off as heterosexuals in environments in which their families and friends are predominantly heterosexual. Many homosexuals never reveal their sexual orientation, and for those who do the average time between a homosexual person's recognition of their sexual orientation and disclosure of it is more than four years.

Acquired immunodeficiency syndrome has been a serious health issue facing the entire world for over four decades, and of sample populations of individuals diagnosed with AIDS in the US in 1993 62% were homosexual males (Friedman & Downey, 1994). Few women in general have

AIDS, and most of the women who contract AIDS do so from heterosexual contact with HIV-positive men. Less than 2% of heterosexual men contracted AIDS from sexual intercourse during 1993. Although the AIDS crisis predominantly affected homosexual males, it affected all members of society, and it has led to an increased homophobia in populations throughout the world in response to the deadly epidemic. Unfortunately, the public has had a tendency to assume that all homosexuals are at an increased risk for contracting AIDS, and both homosexual men and women have had to endure bias from employers, social service departments, insurance companies, and healthcare providers. This has resulted in homosexuals being refused employment, social services, coverage, and medical treatment as a result of an unnecessary fear toward non-heterosexual sexual orientations and AIDS.

Psychiatric problems have resulted from the symptoms caused by those who have contracted HIV as a result of the infections and cancers associated with the disease, and the subsequent disease following HIV transmission often results in neurologic syndromes that decreases motivation, impairs social judgment, and alters mood (Friedman & Downey, 1994). The discrimination that is endured by homosexual people can lead to isolation, but for individuals suffering from AIDS the isolation that results from being chronically ill and shunned by one's support system can be great. The isolation and medical conditions resulting from AIDS cause internalized conflict, which is compounded by the disease process and informing one's immediate family about one's sexual orientation. Homosexual individuals who have AIDS are typically cared for by their lovers, and these individuals are often supported by communities of bereaved who have endured serial losses. The strain placed on relationships as a result of AIDS, and the disease further complicates couples sexual relationships because of fear of infecting their partners. The loss of the sexual dimension of a couple's relationship can result in increased stress and shame for individuals, which is exacerbated by the disease process as a result of the loss of bodily fluids, perceived unattractiveness, and lack sexual interest. Partners caring for individuals who are suffering from AIDS must cope with decisions regarding celibacy and infidelity, which adds further stress on their relationships and ability to care for others. Some studies have reported increased suicide rates among homosexual men with AIDS, but it is unclear if these resulted from psychiatric issues or were rational suicide as a result of the disease. Psychological interventions that have reported success with AIDS patients and their family members are self-help groups, psychotherapy, and pharmacotherapy.

Sexual Orientation

Studies measuring mental pathology have failed to distinguish between the forms of psychopathology in heterosexual and homosexual individuals (Friedman & Downey, 1994). Researchers have found that heterosexual and homosexual individuals have similar psychodynamic motivations despite their differences in sexual orientation, but developmental issues contributing to individuals sexual orientation has been found to be different between them. Individuals on the developmental path to homosexuality have reported having homosexual attraction during their childhoods despite knowing about homosexuality, and homosexual adults typically describe themselves as having felt different from others throughout adolescence. During childhood, homosexual individuals have reported having feelings of shame and self-hatred toward themselves as a result of their sexual orientation. These feelings result from identification with those who devalue them and the psychological mechanisms resulting from abuse. Childhood is a painful experience for many homosexuals, and it is believed to be a contributing factor in the increased rates depression, drug use, and dependence in alcohol seen in homosexuals. Studies across the United States have not shown an increased suicide rate in homosexuals, but studies have shown that homosexual youths have a disproportionately high number of attempted suicides. Investigations of homosexual youths who have attempted suicide shows that many of them have internal conflicts regarding their sexual orientation, and it is believed being homosexual in a predominantly heterosexual society has predisposed these adolescents to attempt suicide. Some researchers feel that the data regarding homosexual suicide rates may be skewed because individuals may have committed suicide and been conflicted about their sexual orientation, but their sexual orientation may have been hidden from others. For this reason, physicians and psychologists must be particularly sensitive to self-hatred displayed by patients in response to conflict feelings resulting from homosexuality and dealing with homophobia.

Most individuals experience confusion regarding their sexual orientation in adolescence, but most adolescents who participate in homosexual activities or have homosexual feelings do not become homosexual adults (Friedman & Downey, 1994). The American Academy of Pediatrics has developed guidelines for physicians and psychologists to assist in helping adolescents in dealing with issues regarding their sexuality and to help culminate positive self-acceptance of their sexual orientation. Of the minority of homosexuals that were once married, many are parents, and over six million children in the US presently have homosexual parents. Research that has been done on same-sex sexual orientation has shown few adverse effects on children's mental stability, sociability, and overall functioning. The frequency of homosexual children produced from homosexual oriented environments is not statistically any greater than that of heterosexual oriented environments, but there has not been much research done on children with homosexual fathers. From the information collected, sexual orientation of parents on the basis of psychiatric or legal decisions should not in itself be used to make decisions regarding parenting or planned parenting. In Western societies, there are increasing numbers of homosexual individuals and couples who are requesting medical assistance to achieve parenthood through reproductive techniques, and it is advised by most psychologists in regards to the data that has been collected on sexual orientation to not base decisions regarding the use of donated gametes and gestational surrogates solely on individuals' sexual preference.

Changing Sexual Orientation

Of individuals seeking a change in sexual orientation, most consider themselves to be homosexual and are attempting to become heterosexual, and they typically seek treatment because of homophobic discrimination and for religious reasons (Friedman & Downey, 1994). There is not a lot of long-term data available on individuals who have received therapy and attempted to change their sexual orientation, and there is little evidence that shows that homosexual fantasies are replaced in individuals who seek sexual orientation changes. Women's sexual fantasies differ from men's, and it has been found that most women are able to experience bisexual fantasies and participated in bisexual activity without having to construct a social role of being homosexual. The patients who seek to change their sexual orientation have diverse sexual attitudes, values, and psychopathological features. The incompatibility between one' sexual desires and personal values can sometimes not be resolved through therapy, and it is important for healthcare professionals working with these individuals to help preserve their self-esteem and help them to avoid becoming depressed.

Homosexuality and Genetics

Deoxyribonucleic acid studies of males have linked genetic inheritance in males to homosexual orientation through the selective studies of families that have aggregates of homosexuality (Friedman & Downey, 1994). This data has also been confirmed with studies of monozygotic and dizygotic twins of both sexes, and the genetic influence of homosexual orientation has also been seen in identical twin studies separated early in life and reared in different environments. Both homosexual men and women have reported increased cross-gender behavior throughout their lives, and researchers have found that most boys with mental disorders regarding gender typically become homosexual as adolescents or adults. Although childhood gender-identity disorder has not been found to be directly influenced by genetic factors, it is still believed by some in the scientific community that prenatal androgen deficit results in homosexuality in males, and that excess prenatal androgens leads to homosexuality in females. There has been a well documented aversion to fighting and rough play adolescence homosexual males, and the opposite pattern in females has been recorded in homosexual females. Studies have shown that brains of heterosexual men and homosexual men differ in areas of the hypothalamus and thalamus. There is also an increased rate of homosexuality in men born in later groups of siblings, which is believed to be a result of prenatal sex hormone secretion. Prenatal hormones levels are influenced by both biological and environmental factors, and prenatal stress has been shown to inhibit the secretion of testosterone in rats and influence their sexual behavior.

Chapter 3: Homosexuality and Law

Prohibitions against homosexual acts exist in eighty nations and territories throughout the world, and individuals may pay with their lives in nearly 10% of these (Asal, Sommer, and Harwood, 2013). Nations with legal systems based on English common law inherited prohibitions against homosexual acts, but many of these have decriminalized sodomy over the last four decades. These prohibitions directly influenced gay rights up to the end of the twentieth century and can historically be linked to colonization of the British Empire. In many of these nations and territories, homosexuality became illegal as they came under control of Britain and the continued prohibition of same-sex relations continued to expand for centuries thereafter. There has been little research done on the political and economic variables that have influenced changes in the legal evolution of gay rights, and most of the research that has been done to date has primarily focused on social liberalization of individuals within society. The legalization of homosexual acts throughout nations is dependent on a wide array of variables, such as: types of legal systems, economic developments, religion, democratic conditions, and globalization. The homosexual rights issues within nations and the illegality of it that exists within some nations is legally intertwined with larger civil liberties protections. Most nations suffer from path dependence, which counteracts changes brought about in regards to modernization through globalization.

An understanding of the forces that effect policies within the 80 nations and territories that have criminalized sexual acts between consenting same-sex partners is crucial to comprehending the subsequent legislation and decriminalization of homosexual activities in other nations throughout the world (Asal, Sommer, and Harwood, 2013). Although homosexuals have gained legal status for their activities and relationships in many nations, it is important to recognize that in most countries homosexuals are still not treated equally to heterosexuals. There were fewer than 30 countries throughout the world that offered civil unions to homosexual couples in 2008, so it is clear that legality cannot be considered the ultimate measure of discrimination within societies. Therefore, a better understanding of cross-national rights can be gained through examining the legality of homosexual activities.

Path Dependence

Path dependence exists within all societies, and it is a dynamic force that continually reinforces processes within a social system (Asal, Sommer, and Harwood, 2013). Path dependence is created through political choices that shape social systems, and alternative social systems typically cease to be available once they are forgone at earlier stages in the process. Legal path dependence is important to understanding the decriminalization of homosexual acts cross-nationally because the legality or illegality is related to the legal system that has been put in place by nations. The illegality of homosexuality can be directly traced to the export of the British common law system from the sixteenth century, and the subsequent judicial decisions and laws passed led to the criminalization of homosexual acts within these nations. In comparison, nations that adopted the French legal system from this period did not have the same effect, and homosexual acts were decriminalized following the French Revolution. As a result, countries that did not adopt British common law and adopted another type of European common law, similar to the French common law system, have been less likely to criminalize same-sex relations throughout history. Once a legal system has been established within a nation, there are two major mechanisms that prohibit change: cost and adaptive expectations.

The cost of setting up a new legal system is prohibitively high, which considerably diminishes the likelihood of implementing new legal systems (Asal, Sommer, and Harwood, 2013). Once a legal system is established, the belief system regarding it is enhanced, and this belief becomes stronger overtime. There is an underlying advantage for already established legal systems because it becomes locked in, and this becomes difficult to change despite there being alternative legal systems available. Following the acceptance of a legal system within a nation, the evolution of it happens within a particular path, and this path becomes a way to narrow legal choices and decision making processes over time. Path dependence is considered to impede dramatic changes and the development of new laws within nations, and one of the main reasons is that there is an interdependence between legal education, legislation, and other major institutions. Implementing changes to a legal system involves reforming legal education and retraining of all staff involved in legal processes. There are some minor laws that are easy to change within every legal system, but the nature of the legal framework of common law is that it has the ability to lock legislation in, specifically laws dealing the economic, moral, and sociopolitical regulations.

Common law's legal framework consists of provisions of constitutions, duties of legislatures, and judicial decisions (Asal, Sommer, and Harwood, 2013). Common law is precedent-based and integrates past legal decisions into law in which each is created into a model, so laws only change marginally as new decisions are reached, which are based on the subject processing of information from a historical context of a system's legal framework. Therefore, decisions that result in changes to a legal framework happen gradually when they do occur, and this is the main reason that the legal status of contemporary political, moral, religious, and economic issues can be difficult to change. Historically, legal acts prohibiting homosexuality in the military date back to the eleventh century in English common law, and the prohibition of homosexual acts is considered to have become entrenched in English common law in the fifteenth century, which made homosexual acts punishable by death. Capital punishment was not removed from the legislation until the nineteenth century, and homosexual acts did not become decriminalized in English common law until the Sexual Offences Act of 1967. In other colonial empires throughout the world that adopted other systems of European common law, homosexual acts have been legal since the eighteenth century, and many of these drafted criminal codes that were not based on religious law, which resulted in the decriminalization of homosexual acts at an earlier periods.

During the Napoleonic Wars, French civil law was adopted during French occupation, and these adoptions took different path dependence than those of nations that adopted British common law from the eighteenth century onward (Asal, Sommer, and Harwood, 2013). Provisions prohibiting homosexual behavior and relationships were absent from French code, so the legal systems that were adopted followed different paths, which ultimately resulted in no prohibition of homosexual acts being entrenched within them. Like all of forms of legal path dependence, systems that adopted French civil law became unlikely to adopt prohibition of homosexuality after the fact because of the high cost of altering legal systems already intact. French code was ultimately adopted and imposed by France, Spain, and the Netherlands on nations that they colonized, and its influence on the manner in which nations dealt with issues of homosexuality was fundamentally different than those that adopted British common law. Legal systems in nations with origins based on socialist and communist ideologies had laws banning homosexual acts prior to their democratization in the 1990s in which homosexual activity became decriminalized. The adoption of the British common law system has not been historically the only variable that has affected laws prohibiting homosexual acts.

Countries that have adopted a state religion are likely to have a legal code that stems from religious principles, and the adoption of these philosophical views when projected onto the formation of laws governing social conduct increases the likelihood of homosexual acts being codified within nations (Asal, Sommer, and Harwood, 2013). An investigation of the adoption of Islam as a state religion has shown that there is typically codified prohibition of homosexual acts in Islamic states in which Sharia law and the Quran are the primary sources for legislation. There are some nations with Muslim majorities, like Indonesia, where Sharia law and the Quran are not used as primary sources for legislative code, and there has been a history tolerating homosexuality within the nation for decades. In many of the Muslim nations with legal codes prohibiting homosexual activity, death is usually imposed as punishment for engaging in such activities. Established legal codes and path dependence offer powerful explanations of why certain nations have not decriminalized homosexual acts. Like other nations with established legal systems, this path dependence will be difficult to change because of the existing equilibrium that has already been established in their legal history. Differing from the path dependence seen in nations that have adopted either British or French common law systems is the added variable of religion, which makes their path dependence more reliant on culture, domestic politics, and religious heritage.

In nations that have decriminalized homosexual acts, the evolution of gay rights has taken different paths on the basis of the type of legal system established within the countries, but the external factors that have influenced change are similar, such as: democracy, minority representation, and globalization (Asal, Sommer, and Harwood, 2013). Major considerations affecting the legality of homosexuality in nations throughout the world are legal structures, democratic conditions, economic developments, and levels of globalization. The effect of democracy on the decriminalization of anti-sodomy laws has been shown to be statistically significant, and in nations in which homosexual acts have been illegal throughout history the biggest influence in the timing of the change of legislation has been democracy. This effect has been found for all nations that have decriminalized homosexuality, regardless of their religious majority.

Legal path dependence in conjunction with colonial heritage play key roles in legal bans on homosexual activity, and the bans of same-sex acts within nations are essentially a result of exogenous factors (Asal, Sommer, and Harwood, 2013). The variables that have resulted in the decriminalization of homosexual acts are globalization and modernity, which can destabilize legal balances within nations that result from path dependence. The origins of the prohibitions of homosexual activity within a nation can be traced to colonial times, and the likelihood of decriminalization of same-sex acts dramatically decreases as a result of path dependence and costs associated with systems based on English common law or when a nation's legal origins stem from Islam. Globalization results in more information on alternative legal institutions being readily available, so it is easier to import legal institutions as are result of the economic, social, and political globalization. Therefore, it is easier for political entrepreneurs and interest groups to change public opinion and increase legal change. In nations that have decriminalized homosexual acts, increased gross domestic product per capita associated with modernization has also been shown to assist in securing the necessary resources to change preexisting legal institutions. Democratic conditions increase the rate of decriminalization of homosexual acts within a nation, but the opposite affect has been shown to occur with religion, specifically Islam. It is not clear whether the decriminalization has been affected more by democratization and globalization or the shift in public opinion that results as populations become more informed of changing global standards. Also, changes in public opinion may be effected by economic development, which indirectly results in institutional evolution as more resources become available for political campaigns. It is clear that past and present global forces have directly influenced legislation, and these have directly impacted the rights and liberties of individuals' sexual acts.

Evolution of Homosexual Legislation

In the twenty-first century, Western countries throughout the world have legalized same-sex acts and registration of homosexual partnerships, which allow same-sex couples to experience the same rights and responsibilities of individuals in heterosexual civil marriages (Lester & Hayes, 2005). The United Kingdom has historically lagged behind other European and Commonwealth nations in decriminalizing and legalizing homosexual acts and civil unions. Early milestones in the UK in legal equality and equal protection under the law were the legal recognition of homosexual rape in 1994, equalizing the age of sexual consent with that of homosexual couples in 2001, and the recognition of homosexual assault as being a "hate crime" in 2003. In countries throughout Europe and North America, same-sex marriage has been legalized, and in other countries throughout Europe and within certain states in America most of the rights and responsibilities have been afforded to same-sex marriages that are experienced by homosexuals. In many parts of the world, homosexuality remains punishable by death, and more than 70 countries in the world entered the twenty-first century with laws that prohibiting same-sex relations.

Debates regarding marriage rights for same-sex couples have been occurring in Western countries throughout the world in recent decades, and it has resulted in Western leaders using the issue to collect social conservative votes from states and provinces within their countries (Lester & Hayes, 2005). Research shows that moral values outweigh issues regarding terrorism, war, and the economy for conservative voters in the United States. Many leaders in the US remain divided on the issue of permitting same-sex marriage, and it has resulted in a battle between state supreme courts and federal supreme courts. Defiance by state supreme courts has caused some states to allow same-sex civil unions prior to imposed decisions by the Federal Supreme Court, and the issue is centralized on the interpretation of states constitutional laws and the interpretation of the definition of civil unions. Arguments for and against permitting same-sex relationships and civil unions arouse strong reactions in all countries, and arguments for and against same-sex marriage range from religious to social. Many individuals hold the inflexible belief that homosexual acts are sinful and morally wrong, so they should be legislatively sanctioned. Although this belief is prejudice, it is difficult to argue against the narrow-mindedness of it, and research has shown that most individuals throughout the world oppose homosexual acts on the basis of religion.

Despite the growing numbers of people who oppose homosexuality being sanctioned through law, religious groups should not theoretically be able to shape laws in modern and secular societies (Lester & Hayes, 2005). In many Western countries throughout the world, same-sex couples have gained the right to register their civil unions and to adopt children, which has further complicated the gay rights debate. Many believe that it is in the best interest of adopted children to be reared by heterosexual couples, and others feel that a homosexual environment that offers emotional and financial stability should appeal to conservatives and faith-based organizations within society because it meets the needs of children needing homes. Many opponents to legislation that allows homosexual partners to enter into civil unions believe that it will undermine the traditional institution of marriage within society, but research from Northern European countries that pioneered homosexual rights within the continent shows that gay couples have not changed their marriage behavior and marriage rates have remained stable since the legislation was enacted. In the region, the number of couples having children in wedlock has not increased, and it is argued by proponents that this is evidence that same-sex civil partnerships strengthen heterosexual marriages because it recognizes and legitimizes the importance of committed relationships within society.

The United Kingdom's Civil Partnership Act and others like it throughout the world is not welcomed by all, but it clearly has been a long overdue reform bringing basic human rights to same-sex couples in accordance with international law (Lester & Hayes, 2005). There is a pressing need throughout the world to bring progressive legislation to homosexuals everywhere to protect and encourage committed same-sex partnerships. Encouraging homosexual couples to live together in stable relationships will benefit their children and society as a whole.

Chapter 4: Homosexuality and Religion

Individuals who argue that homosexuality is morally wrong throughout the world are generally religious devotees, and strong opposition in Western societies on moral grounds has been seen by followers of Abrahamic religions (McBrayer, 2012). In a traditional Christian worldview, there is strong evidence to oppose homosexual behavior in society, and Christians have traditionally appealed to church tradition, scripture, and reason to justify their beliefs. Despite the devotees of Abrahamic religions traditional appeals, these sources provide little clear evidence that homosexual behavior is morally wrong, and it is arguable in some interpretations of the material that it could be considered morally permissible.

The strongest traditional appeal used by Christians is that homosexual behavior is morally wrong because it has been considered to be so traditionally in the church as a result of scriptural interpretation (McBrayer, 2012). Early Christian societies were uncertain about homosexual behavior, and many did not interpret the scriptures as defining homosexual acts as being morally wrong. Prior to the increase of popularity in Europe, homosexual behavior and civil unions were common in Greek and Roman societies. Homosexual behavior was not formally accepted as being morally wrong until the second century with Clement of Alexandria, and the list of church leaders claiming that homosexual behavior was morally wrong since the second century has become long. Opinions offered by these leaders about the immorality of homosexuality varied widely from claims that it was pedophilic to claims stating that it was unnatural. Many church leaders also categorized homosexual acts with other sexual behavior, and sexual acts were interpreted as being immoral if they were not directed toward reproduction. This tradition has continued within the contemporary church, and the official position of the governing authorities within the largest sects of Christianity is that homosexuality is morally wrong. It is natural for Christians to assume that the consistency of official church doctrine over millennia is reason to believe that it is ethically true, especially if it is reinforced by the belief that God works through guiding church leaders.

Despite the impracticality of following tradition in consideration of the contemporary scientific evidence and social benefits of accepting homosexuality, most contemporary Christian arguments against homosexuality appeal to biblical scripture (McBrayer, 2012). One of the underlying problems with interpreting the Bible is that claims regarding morality are made by biblical scholars through analysis of passages in which the word "wrong" is infrequently used. Common citations discussing the immorality of homosexuality used by theologians typically discusses it as being an act that should be considered disgusting or indecent. It is unclear and open for interpretation if the acts that are considered not appropriate should also be considered morally wrong. Homosexual behavior is clearly prohibited in scripture, but the reasons for preventing it are unclear. It is also uncertain if the Bible's discussion forbidding homosexuality was based solely on homosexual acts, or if it was denouncing homosexual acts in reference to male prostitution or sex within temples. Biblical scholars site passages from both the Old Testament and the New Testament in reference to the immorality of homosexual acts, but two of the most popular citations come from the story of Sodom and Gomorrah in Genesis and the Old Testament commandments in Leviticus.

In the story of Sodom and Gomorrah, the homosexual nature of the behavior within the city is not the obvious reason behind God's destruction of the city, and it clearly states that God destroyed the city as a result of Sodom's sister's lack of generosity to the poor (McBrayer, 2012). The sin of Sodom was not engaging in homosexual behavior but of social injustice, and the passage never clearly states that the city was destroyed as a result of Sodom's homosexuality. The law handed down to the people of Israel by Moses recorded in Leviticus has several prohibitions against homosexual acts, but like many of the Old Testament laws there are social regulations set forth that we do not practice in contemporary society. Therefore, if a society only partially upholds Old Testament law, it is difficult to justify homosexuality as being wrong strictly on a theological basis. The Bible is inconsistent in its teaching regarding homosexuality, and it is not obvious in its indications that all homosexual behavior is morally wrong. A society that does not consistently follow the rules set forth in Old Testament law would be inequitably denouncing homosexuals and their acts solely on the basis of biblical scripture.

There is justification to endorse that at least some homosexual behavior is morally permissible because the only difference between heterosexual intercourse and homosexual intercourse is gender (McBrayer, 2012). From a moral standpoint, actions are considered moral or immoral on the basis of the acts and not on the gender of the individual or individuals committing the acts, so acts of homosexual intercourse that are like morally permissible heterosexual intercourse should be considered moral. Therefore, some homosexual intercourse should be considered morally permissible. Since the evidence presented in the Bible can be considered ambiguous and church tradition has provided weak reasoning in support of its disapproval of homosexual intercourse, homosexual intercourse between two consenting individuals who are committed to one another's long-term welfare should be considered morally justified similarly to equivalent heterosexual intercourse. Rejecting homosexual acts on the basis of gender can be considered sexist, especially in consideration of homosexual acts that are as committed similarly to their heterosexual counterparts.

Chapter 5: Homosexuality and Evolution

Homosexuality is a paradox for evolutionists because the adaptiveness of a species behavior is measured by reproductive success (Kirkpatrick, 2000). There is little evidence that species gain reproductive advantages through offspring care given by homosexual members and that homosexuality is a result of kin selection. Therefore, it is believed by most evolutionists that homosexuality is a result of parental control over their offsprings' reproductive decisions, and that homosexuality has arisen as a result of reciprocal altruism or same-sex alliances. There are reproductive advantages in same-sex alliances, and sexual behavior has been shown in many species to be a way to maintain these alliances. Nonhuman primates use homosexuality to maintain same-sex alliances, and it is believed by most evolutionists that these same-sex alliances were important to the distribution of human ancestors during the Pleistocene. Homosexual emotions and behavior emerge as a result of these same-sex alliances.

Homosexual behavior has existed throughout human history, and it is believed by most evolutionists to be present in most human cultures (Kirkpatrick, 2000). The scale of the homosexual experience throughout the world has been well documented through cross-cultural and historical studies. Ten to twenty percent of Melanesian societies require all men to participate in both heterosexual and homosexual sex. In the twentieth century, homosexual partnerships resulted because of a resistance to marriage in China, and the Mpondo miners of South Africa formed homosexual relationships as a result of environmental isolation during the same period. Homosexual behavior was common in other Pacific Island societies prior to

Western influence, and homosexual behavior has been documented in 137 cultures Native American cultures throughout North America prior to European settlement. Homosexual behavior has also been documented in Asia, South America, and pre-colonial Africa. It is estimated that homosexual behavior has been present in nearly 65% of societies throughout the world for certain classes of individuals over the course of human history.

The Darwinian view of human evolution states that individuals should seek to maximize their reproductive success, and since humans reproduce children through mating with members of the opposite sex homosexual acts appear not to help people's reproductive success (Kirkpatrick, 2000). Evolutionists are puzzled by homosexuality because it is widespread enough not to be considered an aberration, and its significance is attached to homosexual relations and not a value-free activity. The underlying assumption regarding homosexual behavior by evolutionists has categorized it as being negative for individual fitness and maintained by indirect selection. Kin-selection theories have been focused on adaptationist explanations in which homosexuals assist with the offspring of relatives, and in the parental-manipulation hypothesis homosexuality results because of parental pressure to forgo reproduction to assist with the offspring of relatives. Other theories have suggested that homosexuality occurs because it is a secondary trait under positive selection. The most plausible theory for contemporary society is that homosexuality occurs because it offers non-conceptive benefits similar to the non-reproductive functions of heterosexual relationships. Homosexual behavior under this view is considered to be a positive selection because maintenance of same-sex alliances can help individuals with competition for resources and cooperative defense. Therefore, homosexual behavior can be viewed as a survival strategy and not a reproductive strategy, and homosexuality can best be explained in reference to the benefits of reciprocal altruism.

Behavior explained through evolution must have inherited components, but homosexuality is a result of both genetic and environmental components (Kirkpatrick, 2000). Culture has consistently been a powerful way to transfer traits between generations, and polymorphic traits have been well documented in humans as a result of mixed strategies used over an individual's lifetime. One of the underlying problems of behavior-based definitions used within research is the restrictiveness of categories used in assigning behaviors to sexually. It, however, is considered to be a better way to classify behavior than self-reports by participants. In a sample of men in the United States, 22% had engaged in homosexual sex, but only 9% reported that they were homosexual or bisexual.

Of the individuals who identify themselves as homosexual, research has shown that the sexual orientation follows family lines, and monozygotic twins have been found to be non-heterosexual at twice the rate of dizygotic twins (Kirkpatrick, 2000). There has also been some evidence of chromosomal concordance in brothers who are not heterosexual, but the studies of both twins and siblings has also shown the importance of environmental factors in contributing to individuals sexual orientation. Of monozygotic male twins reared in the same environments, 52% of those who reported being homosexual also had a twin that was non-heterosexual, and the same was found for 22% of the dizygotic male twins who reported being homosexual. In studies of both male twins and siblings who were adopted and reared in different environments, only 11% of those who reported being homosexual had an adopted male sibling that also reported non-heterosexuality. Therefore, it can be concluded that a large portion of homosexual behavior is free from the influence of genetics and uterine environments.

There is significant evidence that has shown the influence of prenatal hormonal exposure and sexual orientation, which has been seen in the differences of fingerprints between heterosexual and homosexual men (Kirkpatrick, 2000). Fingerprints are a heritable trait, and fingerprint development is completed by the fourth month of pregnancy. There are no apparent differences in androgen receptors between heterosexual and homosexual men, so the evidence regarding prenatal hormones leading to homosexual behavior in men is considered to be inconclusive. There has been a great deal of evidence presented from Western societies that gender-atypical children that display effeminate behavior tend to identify as homosexuals as they become adolescents, but many homosexual populations throughout the world do not have reputations for effeminacy.

Gender nonconformity in behavior cannot be considered necessary for homosexual behavior to occur, and it is clear that sexual orientation is complex and not fully understood (Kirkpatrick, 2000). Prenatal hormones contribute to differences in gender characteristics, and these characteristics may have a tendency to occur with homosexual behavior. The studies that are available on sexual orientation and gender identity lack strict controls for participant groups, and conclusions regarding the data accumulated are invalidated by preconceptions of gender identity. Research has shown that homosexual behavior is connected to social structures, demographics, and birth order. Homosexual behavior has been found to increase by 50% for individuals serving in the military and as a result of public school attendance in England. In North American men, homosexual behavior has been found to result with an increased number of older brothers, and it is believed by researchers to be a result of changes in mothers' immune responses with each new child they conceive, which is hypothesized to mediate the distribution of prenatal hormones. A psychological explanation of the homosexuality and birth order phenomenon results as the opportunities available to males within different positions of family change according to hierarchy and environment for younger male siblings.

Despite the evidence linking homosexual behavior to specific lineages, birth orders, and social networks, there is not a large amount of variation for explanation of any single factor (Kirkpatrick, 2000). Genetics, hormones, and experiences interact to produce individual life histories, and the evidence uncovered to date suggests that all of these weakly correlate and result in the manifestation of homosexual behavior. It is clear that homosexual behavior results from a broad range of influences, and that there are certain groups of traits and experiences that lead individuals to engage in homosexual acts. Sexual behavior and emotions, however, are continuous variables and subject to slight individual differences that lead to homosexual behavior. Thus, it is a mistake to divide individuals into categories that predispose them to homosexual behavior based solely on genetic, hormonal, and environmental factors. Social behaviors are based on a range of established inclinations that are constantly interacting with potential opportunities in environments, so behaviors are dependent on individual conditions that arise for within environments for populations as histories within them accumulate. Therefore, it is clear that sexual behavior is a continuous one ranging from heterosexuality to homosexuality, but it is unclear whether there are two distinct types of sexuality or if sexuality becomes blurred with opportunities presented to individuals within environments. In regards to natural selection, a strategy is not a strategy unless it is implemented, so sexual orientation must be considered a categorical variable.

Over the course of a lifetime, humans typically have few children and invest heavily in each, so our lineage's survival depends more on quality than the total amount of children produced (Kirkpatrick, 2000). If homosexual individuals can adequately improve their reproductive success, it is possible for them to offset their lack of offspring through the virtue of relatedness with individuals who pass common genetic material, like a brother or sister, to the next generation through their successful procreation. This could arise through one's direct support of offspring, direct support of his or her ancestry, or indirectly by not producing competitors within one's lineage. The underlying problem with assuming that homosexuality does not lead to reproductive success is that there is no data to support it. This assumption is based on the biological limitations that are presented through homosexual acts and the inability to physically procreate from them. Most people, however, who engage in homosexual behavior are bisexual, and there has been no compelling evidence produced that suggests that homosexuals have fewer offspring than heterosexuals. Bisexuals in Britain have a higher fertility than heterosexuals before the age of twenty-five, and 83% of homosexual and bisexual men in Japan over the age of thirty have children. In the United States, homosexual women have been found to be childless more often than heterosexual women, and the mean number of children of women reporting homosexual experiences was 1.2 versus 2.2 for women who practiced entirely heterosexual behavior. The success rate in producing offspring for homosexuals clearly is not consistent throughout all societies around the world, but from the data collected homosexuals are successful at reproducing, which correlates with some historical evidence regarding homosexual behavior. In some societies throughout history, most people who produced children also engaged in homosexual behavior, and throughout Asia homosexual behavior has been tolerated throughout history as long as one's heterosexual duties were fulfilled.

Homosexual Behavior

Evolutionists list the possible factors affecting one's reproductive potential as being birth order, sex, and sex ratios within demographics (Kirkpatrick, 2000). In societies with preferences of equality between siblings, individuals with a low birth order typically have less reproductive opportunities than those with a high birth order. In North America, men who identify themselves as being homosexual reported having more older brothers than heterosexual men, and in some societies males with a low birth order are subjected to gender-role reversals in which they were at times raised as females. Males report homosexual behavior at twice the rate of females in the United States, the United Kingdom, and France, which is believed to be directly influenced by the greater variance in reproductive potential and success in a comparison between males and females. The theory that demographics is a factor in influencing homosexual acts, specifically when powerful males have multiple wives and spatial segregation between the sexes exists, is not supported by research data. The underlying assumption in this theory is that homosexual acts primarily occur when heterosexual opportunities are absent, and in some polygynous cultures the opposite is true because at times individuals prefer their same-sex lovers to their husbands or wives.

There are anecdotal accounts throughout history of parental manipulation leading to homosexual behavior as a result of channeling resources or socializing individuals to make them reproductive in heterosexual roles (Kirkpatrick, 2000). In Italy during the fifteenth century, parents encouraged their sons to engage in homosexual relations with individuals from influential families to gain political power, and parents in the fourth century in Byzantium castrated their male sons to qualify for them for positions in court as eunuchs. Trans-gender shamans in North and South American native cultures were chosen as a result of a perceived disposition in childhood and conditioned to serve in the office as adults.

The evolutionary forces that act upon heterosexual relationships are similar in many ways to homosexual relationships, and the forces required to start and to maintain homosexual relationships interfere with the kin selection and parental manipulation theories, which are argued by some evolutionists as evidence for homosexual behavior (Kirkpatrick, 2000). Heterosexual and homosexual people are naturally inclined to invest resources in competing for attraction toward themselves, and the resources and energy invested in a long-term homosexual relationship is similar to heterosexual relationships. The similarity between the two would also extend to the intrasexual competition that exists for both material goods and social support.

Alliance formation of homosexuals that leads to reciprocal altruism distinguishes it from both theories of kin selection and parental manipulation leading to homosexuality because they interfere with each other. Contests for resources of both heterosexual and homosexual individuals all direct selection to act upon the propensity of the behavior, and it is clear that same-sex alliances do assist individuals' survival because homosexual behavior does help with alliance formation.

There is limited data available on the benefits of same-sex alliances with offspring for individuals who have established and maintained households and helped children reach reproductive age (Kirkpatrick, 2000). There is some indirect evidence that men who engage in homosexual alliances may improve their reproductive success because the relationships assist in maintaining social networks and marriage exchanges, which can ultimately increase their survival. Researchers have found that in Belize men that maintain same-sex alliances have significantly more children in comparison to heterosexuals because of increased productivity of agricultural labor. In societies throughout the African continent, female homosexual behavior helps to negotiate social alliances and extend trade networks that help with economic security. There is historical evidence of same-sex unions in North America, Asia, and many other pre-colonial societies in which pair-bonds led to increased food intake and cooperative defense for individuals and their children. This evidence shows that many of these same-sex alliances were age-graded in which a younger partner would accommodate an older through manual labor in exchange for food and education. The social advantages of same-sex unions have been shown in ancient Greek, Melanesian, and Japanese historical records, and individuals who did not participate in these alliances within these cultures were considered to be at a social disadvantage. Same-sex alliances that include homosexual unions have typically displayed exogamy rules and customs similar to those seen in heterosexual relationships, and these same-sex exchanges for both males and females link individuals in complex groups of mutual dependence and social obligation. Same-sex alliances usually involve homosexual behavior, but it is not required for the formation of alliances that entail rights and responsibilities of partners. There is cultural evidence from regions within Africa that these rights and responsibilities of same-sex partnerships, which include both homosexual and celibate individuals, are celebrated in formal ceremonies that include wealth exchanges. For the cultures that do permit homosexual behaviors in these alliances, the sexual behavior of adolescents is predictive of the alliances that are formed and celebrated by communities as adults.

Same-sex alliance formation theories assume that self-motivated homosexual behavior acts to enhance individuals' survival and underlying these theories is the assumption that the engagement of homosexual acts exclusively is maladaptive in Darwinian terms (Kirkpatrick, 2000). Therefore, the number of bisexuals should outnumber homosexuals, which has been demonstrated in contemporary and historical societies throughout the world. Evidence in contemporary North American society suggests that the majority of individuals who self-identify as homosexuals actually practice bisexuality, and there are over two millennia of historical records from China identifying known homosexuals as also participating in heterosexual activity. Throughout the world homosexual attraction has been linked to homosexual emotion although it is not entirely a result of homosexual orientation, and in Australia the majority of homosexual attraction is an emotion expressed by those who predominantly practice heterosexual behavior.

The available evidence does not allow for the rejection of the kin selection, parental manipulation, or the same-sex alliance hypotheses (Kirkpatrick, 2000). Even if a behavior is shown to be adaptive, it does not necessarily mean that it is a product of natural selection. Both the kin selection and parental manipulation hypotheses remain the least satisfying because there is inadequate data available to test their central predictions, and there has been no adequate evidence that homosexual behavior reduces individuals' reproductive success in the majority of people who practice it. Non-reproductive offspring who care for the well-being of their siblings will always benefit their parents' reproductive success, but there is little evidence that in accepting these roles non-reproductive individuals become predominantly homosexual. The present information of parental evaluation of offspring with reproductive potential suggests that parental manipulation results in other behaviors, such as: infanticide, encouraging high-risk strategies, and encouragement of the formation of polyandrous households. Same-sex alliance formation is the hypothesis that best explains observations that have been historically and ethnographically seen because it lacks the requirement that homosexual behavior be detrimental to individuals' reproductive success or benefit individuals' lineages.

Same-sex alliances clearly help individuals survive and reproduce, and bisexual behavior in these alliances is more common than homosexuality (Kirkpatrick, 2000). Same-sex alliance formation also best explains the genetic and developmental correlation with homosexual behavior because homosexual behavior is engaged in during certain stages of individuals' lives in most societies. In mutually dependent animals with repeated contact, reciprocal altruism often develops, and it is important to form alliances with one's partner when there is increased competition for resources. The benefits and costs of reciprocal altruism are complex, and they vary with demographic and ecological conditions. The benefits occur within a short period in alliances formed between peers, but the alliances between younger and older individuals result in benefits that potentially span many generations. For younger individuals in alliances, they are typically entering an already established household that has an intact reproductive system within it, and these individuals become limited by access to both knowledge and resources that permitted the establishment of the household. In these environments, non-reproductive sex has little worth because of the lack of acceptance from other members of the reproductive population within it. Relationships between younger and older individuals are more common in males than females, and it is believed to be a result of increased intrasexual competition between males for access to mates. Pressure for alliances is believed to occur when individual productivity is increased through assisted labor and when there is a great deal of competition for resources. Increased productivity, however, can be detrimental to individuals' reproductive success when additional children produce less benefit than investing in children already produced. Therefore, it is likely that same-sex alliances are seen in greater numbers in societies in which in the investment in offspring is strongly correlated with reproductive success. These societies typically have laws penalizing illegitimacy, predictable environments, and populations near maximum capacities.

Culture is believed to be a greater influence on homosexual behavior than ecology, but individuals' expression of homosexuality is believed to be influenced by ecological variables as well (Kirkpatrick, 2000). Same-sex alliances are typically based on considerations of labor in societies in which labor increases productivity, and same-sex alliances may be structured according to status differentials in societies in which labor increases productivity. Homosexual behavior has been shown to be positively correlated with a low population density in Melanesia, and in a study of 70 cultures throughout the world homosexual behavior has been found to occur more often in agricultural groups and larger social groups. This supports evidence that homosexual behavior is more frequent when prime social forces are political networks and not independent individuals. Throughout history, parental manipulation has been used to exploit both adolescents' reproductive abilities and sexual orientation to establish and maintain alliances. Parents used their sons' sexuality to establish bonds with more powerful households throughout the Mediterranean in the fifteenth century, and in many cultures daughters have been considered assets to their fathers and bestowed on allies to improve their own welfare. Parents have sold both their sons and daughters into indentured prostitution in Japan, and initiation of these practices begins before puberty in societies and can be considered to be pedophilic in the initial stages. Parents clearly have an incentive to manipulate offsprings alliances and use children for their own purposes when these partnerships result in a transfer of wealth to them. Alliances can be maintained without sexual behavior, but sexual behavior is important in maintaining alliances when commitment to social partners is important or competition for partners is severe. Sexual behavior can be considered a currency of long-term supportive relationships and is a way of conferring pleasure, and it can be used to signify to one's partner and others a high level of association. Homosexual acts are powerful symbols of loyalty and affiliation and can be considered adaptive because of the cost in maintaining an alliance. The majority of humans and other primates sexual behavior has direct conceptive benefits, and it remains unclear why sex is used to negotiate and maintain alliances that do not have conceptive benefits. As long as enough heterosexual matings occur in which an individual is provided with an average number of offspring, homosexual behavior cannot be considered to be a selective disadvantage. It is considerably unlikely that homosexual behavior results in a decrease to an individual's reproductive success, specifically in societies that require heterosexual marriages.

Human homosexual behavior has shown similarity across board geographic regions, and it appears to be part of human behavioral repertoire for at least the last 12,000 years (Kirkpatrick, 2000). Organized homosexual behavior is believed to have reached Melanesia 10,000 years ago, and some of the widely divergent cultures across the Americas have displayed ways of incorporating transgender and homosexual behavior into their societies, which suggests that the original human migrants to the continents 12,000 years ago had similar cultures. Homosexual behavior is as frequent as heterosexual behavior in some species of primates, and the strongest adaptive explanations of homosexual behavior in nonhuman primates appears to be the maintenance of social relationships. This homosexual behavior is seen in primates throughout the world in alliances involving aggressive disputes, and it has resulted from imbalances in demographic sex ratios in others. Often, this homosexual behavior results in exchange networks that link sex to food, and it is used to solidify alliances with both high-ranking resident males and females.

Current interpretation from archaeological evidence of early hominids suggests that individuals' success was based on alliances of both sexes, and same-sex alliances are presently considered to be a key aspect of human evolution (Kirkpatrick, 2000). Humans have expanded their geographic distribution over time directly as a result of cooperative behaviors, separation of male and female activities, and through the transfer of knowledge from generation to generation. Over time, it is believed that this should result in a psychological predisposition for same-sex affiliation and would indirectly result in homosexual behavior as part of a complex network of reciprocal exchange, which is present in all Hominidae. From a natural selection point of view, homosexual behavior can be considered adaptive within certain social contexts. Social conditions throughout history have altered the cost and benefits of various behaviors, which explains why alliance formation and homosexual behaviors have been adaptive throughout history in various societies. The cost and benefits of alliances in conjunction with sexual behavior are dependent on dominance hierarchies within families and societies. There is a wide cross-cultural variation in the amount and type of homosexual behaviors because most individuals conform to social norms. Gender socialization in adolescence does not typically counteract hormonal changes that lead to an attraction of the opposite sex, and adolescent homosexual behavior has not been found to be an adequate predictor of adult homosexual behavior. There have been societies in which social norms required men to find other men sexually attractive throughout history, and it is only through recent historical contact that these longstanding social norms have been slowly replaced through contact with Western cultures. Individuals with a strong inclination toward heterosexuality or homosexuality may find it difficult to conform to the requirements of social norms. Homosexual emotion and behavior are clearly tools of alliance formation, which suggests that human sexuality has elements that are common to all primates.

Homosexual behavior is useful for all primates as a form of exchange, and it is traded as a currency similar to heterosexual behavior in forming social alliances (Kirkpatrick, 2000). In analyzing the evolutionary origins of homosexuality, it is impossible to focus entirely on the reproductive functions of sex acts, and scientists will be able to better explain the evolution of homosexuality once data is collected on how the varying degrees of bisexuality affect individuals' reproductive success. Further genetic, hormonal, and family research must be conducted to determine the dynamics that are exclusive to individuals' sexual orientation. It is clear that there are different human experiences that lead to increased and decreased tendencies to form alliances with members of the same-sex, and these alliances are affected by social and cultural constraints that influence decisions regarding how sexual behavior is used to secure and maintain them. The evolution of homosexuality in humans is tied to the benefits of same-sex affiliation, and both sexes have the ability to form affectionate bonds with the same-sex to varying degrees. Attraction to members of the same-sex is no way perverse in comparison to attraction to members of the opposite sex, and homosexuality is a quality for individual selection of same-sex affiliation that has been part of human and primate experience since its beginning.

Chapter 6: Genetics and Environment

Homosexuality has been found to be linked to fraternal birth order by researchers, and it links male homosexuality to biological factors that are present before birth (Bogaert, 2006). Prior to this research, scientists have speculated about the link between fraternal birth order and homosexuality, but it was unclear if this phenomenon was a product of prenatal mechanisms or a result of the socializing effect of having older brothers on individuals' sexuality. The causes behind fraternal birth order and male homosexuality have shown a direct correlation between the number of biological older brothers a male has and his sexual orientation. The effect has been scientifically attributed to maternal memory for male births, and it has only been shown for biological brothers and not adopted siblings. Therefore, the number of biological brothers, including those raised in other environments, increases the likelihood of homosexuality in younger males who are biologically related.

In the last four decades, Western societies have seen an increased social and legal acceptance of homosexuality, but with this increased acceptance there has been an increase in the causes behind the development of individuals' sexual orientation (New England Newspaper, 2013). To date, there have been many hypotheses proposed and research studies conducted regarding homosexuality, and a great deal of the research that has been conducted to the present has led many to speculate about whether researchers will eventually locate a gene or a group of genes, which can be directly attributed to individuals sexual orientations. Scientific research conducted on individuals' sexual orientations has not presently led to a definitive answer regarding whether individuals sexual orientations are a result of nature or nurture. Therefore, concerned individuals must conclude that at this point individuals' sexual orientations are a result of influences from both nature and nurture. The only aspect of homosexuality that current research has shown is incorrect is that homosexuality is a choice.

There is definitive evidence that individuals' sexual orientation is affected by genes inherited by mothers who bear many children, and research evidence has shown increased rates of homosexuality in men who have women in their immediate and extended families that produce high numbers of offspring (New England Newspaper, 2013). There has also been some genetic evidence linking the change of a woman's immune system during the birthing of her eldest sons, which increases the likelihood of homosexuality by 20% in younger male offspring. The current genetic research concerning homosexuality produces some definitive evidence that links individuals genetics with sexual orientation, but individuals' sexual orientations still cannot be entirely be attributed to their genetic inheritance.

Individuals' environments will affect their sexual preferences, and it is logical to attribute individuals' sexual preferences to where and how they grow up (New England Newspaper, 2013). Individuals reared by homosexual parents will directly be imprinted with the concept that homosexuality is acceptable, which would indirectly lead to the questioning of their own sexuality and increase the possibility that they would be attracted to the same-sex. Individuals that have homosexual parents have an increased probability of being homosexual themselves.

Researchers have long speculated about individuals who are sexually assaulted as children, and it is currently believed by some scientists that repeated sexual assault in childhood can lead to increased homosexuality because of the continued repression and confrontation of past traumatic experiences. This is believed to potentially lead a victim toward or away from a particular sex because of the subsequent experience or experiences that occurred in their childhood or as a young adult. There are clearly multiple ways that one's environment can influence their sexual orientation despite their former traumatic experiences not being individual choices.

It can be concluded that both nature and nurture contribute to individuals' sexual orientations because some people are born homosexual and others are conditioned to be attracted to the same-sex (New England Newspaper, 2013). Presently, it is impossible to offer a single reason for individuals' sexual preferences, and people do not make conscious choices regarding their sexual orientations. Genetics does play a part in individuals' sexual orientation, but there are many factors that affect individuals' sexuality.

The Homosexuality Controversy

One of the most controversial scientific and social issues in the twenty-first century is homosexuality and its origins, and despite the evidence that homosexuality is practiced in more than 1,500 species the majority of religious authorities and political institutions consider it to be unnatural (Jannini et al., 2010). Homosexuality is natural, but it is presently unclear the level of biological influence and environmental influence that leads to the development of individuals sexual orientations. There is a great deal of research that supports that biology is an important regulator of all sexual behavior, and there has been evidence produced that shows the importance of genetic, autoimmune, and neurohormonal factors in the development of individuals sexual orientations. There has not been any research that has produced compelling evidence of set of genes connected to individuals' sexual orientations, but genetic research using families and twins has shown a consistent influence of genetic influence on individuals' sexual orientations.

It has been well established that the odds of homosexuality in men are increased when individuals have older brothers, but the reasons behind it have not been entirely scientifically resolved (Jannini et al., 2010). The proposition of the gene homosexuality in males solved the Darwinian paradox of how an anti-reproductive gene could survive the fertility disadvantages of carrying the gene. Genetic homosexuality in males has been compared to thalassemia, which offers protection against malaria in regions where the trait is common. Therefore, genetic homosexuality in males may offer selective survival advantages on carriers who perpetuate the mutation similarly to group of hemolytic diseases caused by faulty hemoglobin synthesis, which is also passed on through genetic inheritance.

The morphofunctional research that has been conducted on homosexuality in males suggests that it is a result of brain "feminization" caused by maternal antibodies, and male homosexuality has been attributed to autoimmune feminization during fetal life in some cases (Jannini et al., 2010). This research has been supported by evidence of hypothalamic activation in response to male pheromones in homosexual males, which is similar to that of heterosexual females. This has been shown only to work for homosexual males with older brothers, and the pattern has been shown only as a consequence of individuals' sexual interest of the same gender and not a cause of individuals' sexual orientation. Propositions that homosexual males are incompletely masculinized as a result of the morphofunctional research showing hypothalamic activation similarity between homosexual males and heterosexual females have been put into question as a result of hormonal levels and dimorphic traits. Hypersexuality is more present in homosexual male populations in comparison to heterosexual male populations, and homosexual males have been shown to have higher testosterone levels than heterosexual males. Genital sizes in homosexual males have been shown to be larger than heterosexual males, and homosexual males with older brothers have shown to have a 2D and 4D finger length ratio that is indistinguishable from heterosexual males. The role of hormones in homosexual male behavior is clearly hyperandrogenic rather than hypogonadal.

There have been some methodological weaknesses in the research evidence produced by scientists regarding the influence of nature on male homosexuality, but there has been enough replicable evidence to state definitively that male homosexuality is influenced by genetic, autoimmune, and neurohormonal factors (Jannini et al., 2010). The research has also made it clear that male homosexuals are clearly not a homogenous group, which offers support to researchers who believe that homosexuality is a result of environment despite there being little verifiable evidence to support their claims. An important theoretical difference between the natural and environmental theorists is that naturalists do not exclude the influence environmental factors contributing to male homosexuality. The psychosexual neutrality theory is based on environmental influence on individuals' sexuality, and it proposes that all individuals are psychosexually neutral at birth and sexual orientation is a consequence of the nurture received during childhood. Underlying this theory is the assumption that homosexuality is a disease and treatable through psychotherapy, but there is no scientific evidence that an individual's sexual orientation can be converted through psychotherapy. Despite the lack of scientific evidence, psychotherapists have reported success in changing both male and female homosexual behavior through the identification of typical behavior patterns in homosexuals, but complete shifts in both male and female homosexuals' behavior were found to be uncommon. Homosexuality has been removed from the "Diagnostic and Statistical Manual of Mental Disorders" for good reason, and it is clear that homosexuality cannot be cured because it is not a disease.

The effect of increased rates of male homosexuality as a result of birth order in younger human males is referred to as the fraternal birth order effect (Jannini et al., 2010). The increased odds of male homosexuality have not been found for other classes of siblings, and it has not been consistently shown to increase the rates of homosexuality in human females. Studies on male homosexuality in younger brothers have demonstrated a wide variety of populations in which male homosexuality has been statistically associated with having older brothers. Each additional older brother increases a male's odds of homosexuality by 33%, and some estimates of the prevalence male homosexuality in the general population it at roughly 2% for males without any older brothers. This places male homosexuality as a result of fraternal birth order as the number one cause of homosexuality in males with three or more older brothers. This effect has been found to result in biological brothers who are reared in different households, and it has not been found for individuals reared with stepbrothers or adoptive brothers, which suggests that the phenomenon is prenatal. The fraternal birth order effect on male homosexuality led to the maternal immune hypothesis to explain the biological action behind the occurrence. The maternal immune hypothesis proposed that the production of antibodies by a mother's immune system as a result of maternal circulation of male cells causes anti-male antibodies to enter male fetuses' brains. In this instance, a mother's immune system recognizes male-specific cells as foreign and produces antibodies, which cross the placental barrier and enter the brains of male fetuses. These antibodies are believed to divert sexual differentiation of fetal brains from male-typical pathways, and the result is that individuals are later attracted to other males instead of females. The probability of maternal immunization increases with each subsequent male fetus, so homosexuality increases with each older brother for human males. This hypothesis was never intended to account for the sexual orientation of all homosexual men, and over 50% of homosexual men do not have any older brothers. It is estimated that other etiological factors account for more that 70% of the occurrence of male homosexuality in the general population, which include genes and atypical hormonal levels during different stages of fetal development.

It is estimated that 180 to 200 million individuals throughout the world exhibit a homosexual orientation, and there have been recent popularized rehabilitative therapies discussed in the media to cure homosexuality despite a lack of scientific evidence supporting the treatments (Jannini et al., 2010). These treatments offer cures for homosexuality through psychoanalysis, group therapy, and spiritual healing, and they have been censured by the American Psychological Association because they were non-evidence based and believed to be potentially harmful. Empirical evidence suggests that homosexuality is adaptive and beneficial, which is evidence in the maternal fertile female theory. The maternal fertile female hypothesis has shown that families with homosexual members reproduce more than families without homosexual members, which was supported by evidence that ascendant female members of maternal lines with homosexual members were more fertile than ascendant female members of maternal lines of heterosexual members. This research suggests that there are dynamic factors influencing homosexuality, and that homosexuality contributes to maternal line fertility in populations. Furthermore, homosexuality should be considered a natural aspect of human sexual variability and not a pathological disorder that can be cured.

Explanations for homosexuality throughout history have varied from it being considered a pathological disorder to present explanations, which attempt to offer scientific evidence in support of the phenomenon under varying degrees of bias (Jannini et al., 2010). Individuals' sexual identities are formed during puberty through the integration of three independent entities: one's gender identity, one's capacity for relationships, and one's sexual responsiveness. In childhood, these entities are relatively isolated, but they begin to interact in puberty and lead to the formation of individuals' sexual orientation. Gender identity is a key factor influencing one's sexual orientation, and boys who display gender non-conformity have an increased likelihood of ending up with homosexual identities. It is not clear of whether or not gender non-conformity leads to one's homosexual identity because it is impossible to know if one's gender non-conformity leads to isolation by peer group members or if it is a result of developmental factors leading to both gender and sexual identity. The proposition that homosexuality is a form of hormonal intersex has been refuted for the most part, but there has been some limited evidence showing that homosexual men's brain processing to olfactory cues is similar to that of heterosexual women. It is not clear whether this is an innate brain difference in homosexual men or if it is a learned pattern that follows individuals' establishment of homosexual identities. Although one's capacity for relationships is considerably important to his or her development of a sexual identity, there has not been any considerable research in its contribution to sexual orientation. Children vary in the age in which they begin to experience sexual arousal, but there has been some evidence that pre-homosexual males begin to have sexual attraction slightly earlier than pre-heterosexual males. This opens the possibility that the experience of sexual attraction at an earlier age may increase the likelihood of males developing same-sex attraction. Individuals' conditionability to specific stimuli is considered to be an additional factor in the development of sexual orientation, which has been shown to have a striking variance between genders. Males have been found to have more unusual forms of sexual preference in comparison to females, and this is consistent with theories suggesting that sexual attraction is stimulus specific in men and determined by relationship factors in women. The extent in which conditionability influences individuals' sexual identities is not known yet, but it may only be relevant to a minority of individuals.

All of the determinants considered thus far are believed to be genetically influenced, which has been shown through investigations of families, twins, and genetic markers (Jannini et al., 2010). The rate of homosexuality in brothers is 9%, which is higher than the prevalence in general population samples. Also, monozygotic twins have consistently shown across studies to have higher rates of homosexuality than dizygotic twins. Both of these findings support genetic and environmental influences on rates of homosexuality. Finally, the identification of the gene Xq28 in the region of the X chromosome has been attributed to homosexuality in males, but it is presently believed that this association of homosexuality with a specific gene can only account for a fraction of the overall heritability of homosexuality. In respect to the complexity of individuals' sexual orientation, individuals' sexual identities are presently believed to result from numerous genes by most geneticists.

The process of integrating the independent entities of individuals' gender identities, capacities for relationships, and sexual responsiveness into sexual identities is influenced by sociocultural factors (Jannini et al., 2010). Cultural anthropologists divide this pattern of integration into continuous and discontinuous developmental factors, which have been found to vary significantly across cultures. The discontinuous pattern involves a series of sequential stages that vary in degrees of awareness and involvement by both family and society, but the pattern is considered to have the most relevance in demonstrating sociocultural influence on homosexuality. The best anthropological evidence of this is in the Sambia tribe from Papua New Guinea in which male tribesmen pass through a phase of homosexual activity and into a final phase of heterosexual activity. This homosexual phase from adolescence into young adulthood is strongly supported by a sex-segregated society in which males are taken from their mother's at the age of 10 and made to live in all male dormitories. During this phase of the male adolescents lives in which they are placed in a dormitory, they are made to practice homosexual acts, and upon the completion of puberty are made to leave the dormitory to begin a heterosexual life, which eventually leads to heterosexual marriage. In Western societies, researchers have seen discontinuous patterns of homosexuality throughout the twentieth century. In the first half of the twentieth century, researchers found that over 35% of men reported homosexual experiences in early adolescence, which was found to decline in the latter half of the twentieth century as a result of increased opportunities for heterosexual interaction by adolescent males. The Gay Rights Movement that emerged in Western societies in the 1960s and 1970s is believed to have created a social distinction in homosexual and heterosexual identities. The influence of the Internet at the end of the twentieth century and the beginning of the twenty-first century has resulted in the facilitation of an increased range of sexual identities. Although homosexual interactions are common across many species, exclusive homosexual involvement that results in rejection of heterosexual activity is rare in nonhumans. There are no clear scientific determinants of homosexuality, but research has indicated that there are a number of factors influencing same-sex interaction and attraction, which include sociocultural influences on individuals' sexual identity formations.

Chapter 7: Homosexuality in Nature

Homosexual behavior is seen in more than 450 animal species throughout the world, and it has been found in every major geographical region and animal group on Earth (Grant, 1999). Homosexual behavior has been identified in animals in pair-bonding, parenting, and sexual displays. The animal kingdom is full of heterosexual, homosexual, and bisexual creatures, and the biological frequency of occurrence non-heterosexual behavior in animals throughout the world is clearly a lot more widespread than most individuals realize. This has large ramifications for research being done on homosexuality in humans because it is not possible to solely attribute it to cultural and historical influences. It is clear that homosexuality is a part of a biological quality that can be attributed to many species on Earth, and the same biological and environmental forces that influence sexuality in humans occurs in many other animal species. Biologists in the past have been hesitant to attribute same-sex behavior in animal species to homosexuality because of heterosexual bias, but the acts are clearly open to interpretation. The same-sex acts seen in a wide variety of animals of both sexes have shown animals engaging in homosexual behavior that results in genital rubbing, which is coupled with expression and signs of enjoyment. One of the analytical problems with interpreting animal social behavior as homosexuality is that biologists interpreting it as behavior similar to humans are directly projecting human value systems on animals. The main argument against homosexuality in animals is that it does not fit into Darwin's theory on natural selection in which animals are driven by the need to eat and reproduce. Clearly, the same evolutionary theory that has become some people's justification for not accepting homosexuality in humans has confronted biologists in their interpretation of animal social behavior. Similarly to humans, homosexuality may be found to be an adaptive strategy in reinforcing social bonds in animals.

Ruminant Mounting

Male-to-male mounting is well documented in ruminant species despite being inconsistent with the laws of nature (Ungerfeld et al., 2013). Research has shown that some ruminant species are male-oriented, which can be partially explained by genetic trends and brain differences. Testosterone is the main sex hormone related to male sexual behavior, and research has shown that testosterone levels are higher for ruminant species with female-oriented members in comparison to male-oriented members. Despite there being little scientific data, it is widely accepted by biologists that male homosexual behavior in ruminant species is related to social hierarchies, and that dominance is imposed through homosexual mating. Other researchers consider male homosexual behavior as a component of sexual behavior and not as a type of aggression because often hierarchical relationships cannot be distinguished in groups of males, and male-to-male mounting increases in frequency when female members are in estrus. Homosexual mating and mounting appear to have a positive relationship in hierarchical positions between males in herds, and they are a normal process in the maturational process of male ruminants.

Male ruminants reared in environments in which they have permanent contact with females display increased sexual activity in comparison to those raised in isolation from females, and ruminants that display a high sexual activity level within male groups have displayed a preference for males over estrous females when used for breeding (Ungerfeld et al., 2013). For male ruminants raised in isolation from females, their preference of male ruminants over females when breeding is believed to result because of a limited sexual capacity in which they only recognize other male ruminants as potential sexual partners. Research has shown that male ruminants raised with female ruminants consider other male ruminants less sexually attractive than male ruminants raised in isolation with other male ruminants. Male ruminants raised in same-sex groups have increased homosexual interests in comparison to male ruminants raised in heterosexual groups, and some male ruminants raised in isolation developed individual sexual attachments with other males. Homosexual behavior in ruminant species thought to be a result of hierarchy establishment between males is clearly an interaction of sexual origin and not solely a display of dominance.

The testosterone levels of male ruminant species is affected by situations that increase stress, and when mixing groups of male ruminants that had been raised in isolation and those raised in heterosexual environments testosterone levels increased were shown to increase (Ungerfeld et al., 2013). Sexual behavior, however, displayed by male ruminant species cannot not be explained by differences in testosterone levels because heterosexual ruminant behavior is not dependent on testosterone levels and male-to-male ruminant mounting occurs throughout the year. Therefore, the sexual behavior displayed by male ruminant species is not directly related to testosterone levels, and the increased sexual behavior of both heterosexual and homosexual male ruminant species is more dependent on the level of sexual stimulation than testosterone levels.

The environment in rearing of male ruminant species influences mating practices, and male ruminant species raised in isolation from females will display increased mating behavior towards other males in comparison to males raised in heterosexual environments (Ungerfeld et al., 2013). The differences displayed between male ruminants are not a result of testosterone levels but their environments, which directly impacts male ruminants' sexual preferences. The implications of this are significant for breeding programs involving male ruminant species.

Evolutionary Consequences

Homosexual behavior in animals has fascinated scientists and non-scientists for millennia, but there has been little research done on the evolutionary consequences and the circumstances under which homosexuality occurs in various animals species (Bailey & Zuk, 2009). The variety of homosexual behavior in animals is wide-ranging and impressive, and there are thousands of instances of various forms of sex-courtship, pair bonding, and copulation in animals throughout the world. These behaviors are seen in all types of animals: mammals, birds, reptiles, amphibians, insects, and nematodes. Scientists throughout history have typically underestimated the frequency of homosexual interactions in animals being observed because of the assumption regarding pairs being sexually monomorphic in species engaging in sexual behaviors. Same-sex behavior in animals has puzzled researchers because it is considered to be non-adaptive, and it has been a persistent and well-documented across nearly all taxonomic groups. There are, however, few examples of lifelong pairings occurring in animals, and it is clear that when viewed from a larger framework same-sex behavior in animals can only be considered an adaptive strategy, which has led to evolutionary consequences that most biologists have not considered.

Same-sex behavior is prevalent in enough animals to have a significant influence on the social dynamics of wild populations in many species (Bailey & Zuk, 2009). In dolphins, over 50% of sexual interactions are male-to-male mounting, and colonies of birds throughout the world have shown female-to-female pair bonding in populations that have a large number of females, which resulted in rearing success of chicks similar to heterosexual pairs. It is clear that same-sex pair bonding is a flexible breeding strategy that females could use in response to fluctuations in sex-ratios in populations, which then may alter the social structure and interactions within populations and may impact the evolutionary dynamics of them. It is clear that in certain species same-sex pairing increases fitness benefits of members, especially for females because they participate in extra-pair copulations and provide care for their offspring in same-sex pairing. This also decreases the likelihood of separation of male-female pairs because same-sex pairing removes excess females, so there is less pressure for males to abandon their partners for other female members. There are potential evolutionary consequences resulting from the willingness of females to pair bond with each other in a species because population levels within species becomes codependent on females' willingness to form same-sex pairs to rear young.

Future research in same-sex behavior in animals should focus on their evolutionary effects, specifically the indirect genetic effects that they have on populations (Bailey & Zuk, 2009). These indirect genetic effects result from one individual altering the traits of another individual through social interaction or as a result of modifying the environment to influence another's traits. Individuals influenced by same-sex behavior may experience either increased or reduced reproductive fitness, which can either strengthen or weaken evolutionary responses to natural selection. Same-sex behavior can be viewed as a trait that is shaped by natural selection and a force that influences the selection process.

The sexual selection process among animal species is characterized by competitive interactions that result in increased variation of mating success and reproductive fitness (Bailey & Zuk, 2009). These competitive interactions are either intrasexual or intersexual, and they express themselves in interactions between the sexes in instinctive ways. Same-sex interactions in the animal kingdom result in displays of dominance between males and the mimicking of female behaviors by males, which increase the reproductive fitness of the male members that are exhibiting them. If there is a heritable genetic component to these behaviors, the overall effect will exaggerate or diminish the responses to the selection of traits involved in the behaviors displayed in the interactive process.

The only distinction between same-sex behaviors and other behaviors is that they are sexual, so the evolutionary origins of same-sex behavior should be separated from their present purpose (Bailey & Zuk, 2009). The evolutionary origins of same-sex behavior have the same consequences regardless of their causes, and same-sex behavior once established in an animal species becomes a selective force, which can shape aspects of a species physiology, social behavior, and morphology. A key feature of same-sex behavior in animals is that they are deployed in various ways: as alternatives to traditional reproductive tactics, as cooperative breeding strategy, and to facilitate social bonding.

Chapter 8: Homosexuality and the Brain

Scientists seeking to locate differences between heterosexual and homosexual brains operate under the premise that the brain is a sexually dimorphic structure, areas of the brain display differences between the sexes, and dimorphism leads to functional and behavioral differences between males and females (Vittoria & Robinson, 2000). It is also assumed by scientists attempting to locate the differences between heterosexual and homosexual brains that homosexuals display intersexual behavior and brain structures similar to those of the opposite sex. This places homosexuality in the category of being a gender dysfunction, and it assumes that certain brain markers in individuals can be used to predict their sexual orientation. The issue of using brain markers to identify one's sexual orientation is complex because there are homosexuals in societies throughout the world who have heterosexual nuclear families and sexual relationships with the same-sex outside of their marriages. Brain function is directly shaped through a society's values and an individual's behavior, and each brain responds differently to input, which results in the processing of information in diverse ways depending on an individual's values and priorities. Establishing brain markers to identify individuals' sexuality would not necessarily lead to increased social acceptance of homosexuals, and it could potentially lead to increased bigotry of homosexuals because scientific evidence could be used to justify the prejudice and to view homosexuality as a biological contamination. The origins of homosexuality and biological markers are only of interests to scientists because it is a stigmatized behavior, and research over the last couple of decades has led the public to believe that complex behaviors can be reduced to single genes. The scientific community entered the twenty-first century misleading the public regarding casual links between individuals' sexual orientations, areas of the brain, and sets of genes.

Neurobiology represents a scientific interface between behavior and genetic influence, and it is the science poised to establish links between human behavior and circuitry within the brain (Vittoria & Robinson, 2000). There are many hierarchical levels that exist between the structure of the human brain and behavior, so it is imperative that neuroscientists understand the complexities and implications of research attempting to establish connections between brain structures and homosexuality. Neuroanatomists use morphometric analyses to measure specific regions, groups of cells, and single cells within the human brain. This provides important information regarding the organization of specific areas and patterns within the brain. There is, however, an important distinction between structure and function within the brain, so morphometric analyses do not provide any functional information regarding the brain. Therefore, the anatomical differences found through morphometric analyses could have no impact on the network properties of specific cerebral circuitry. It is unknown if anatomical differences in areas of the brain or groups of areas lead to important functional deviations or not. It is possible that different anatomical structures within the brain perform the same functions.

Studies of the planum temporale and the corpus callosum over the last forty years have resulted in the acceptance of scientific discoveries when structures and functions are combined (Vittoria & Robinson, 2000). Studies in the 1970s reported that portions of the temporal lobe is larger on the left side in the majority of individuals, and that there were differences in the proportions of male and female participants showing this reversed asymmetry. Since this scientific evidence has been presented, these studies have been repeatedly cited to show anatomical difference between heterosexuals and homosexuals, and they have been used to validate morphometric analyses of homosexuals' brains. The corpus callosum, which is a thick group of nerves between the cerebral hemispheres of the brain, has been measured in numerous studies by neuroanatomists because it is believed to be involved in integrating the performance of tasks between the two hemispheres. This area has been measured for differences between male and females, but the results have been inconsistent and non-replicable to date. Despite the generalizations undertaken in the anatomical approach to sexual dimorphism, research by neurobiologists has continued in the twenty-first century in an attempt to locate size differences in specific areas of the brain between heterosexuals and homosexuals. Most of the research has been on the hypothalamus because it is believed to control sexual and reproductive behavior in humans, but it is important to note that the hypothalamus is responsible for many functions and many are still unknown to researchers. The assumption that the hypothalamus is involved in sexual and reproductive behavior in humans is based on reports from the late 1970s that the aggregate of cells in the hypothalamus is larger in male rats than female rats, which is believed to be controlled by male androgens. Similar areas of the hypothalamus have been extensively studied in humans, and differences between sexes and those with multiple sexual orientations resulted in inconclusive findings. Other studies have examined different areas of the brain, and claims have been made regarding the findings of other areas of the brain between the sexes and those with multiple sexual orientations. The findings, however, have not been reproducible to date, so claims that homosexuals brains are similar to the opposite the opposite sex have not been scientifically proven. Neuroanatomical analyses of the human brain to date have demonstrated that heterosexual and homosexual brains are organized identically.

Claims regarding anatomical differences between heterosexual and homosexual brains have led to research being conducted by neurobiologists regarding the influence of hormones and other factors that are believed to change cellular structure during critical stages of brain development (Vittoria & Robinson, 2000). Research on laboratory animals has shown that exposure to different sex hormones at early stages of brain development induce mating behavior, affects gender selection of mates in adulthood, and can drastically change the structure of certain areas of the brain. This has led to the neurobiological hypothesis that exposure to high levels of androgens in utero results in male heterosexuality and female homosexuality, and that low levels of androgens in utero lead to male homosexuality and female heterosexuality. Underlying this hypothesis is the implication that the underlying brain circuitry involved in sexual orientation is fixed following development, and it is unable to be changed in adult life.

The human brain is complex and made up of cells that communicate with each other to integrate information, and the function of the cells within it depends on the expression of thousands of different genes that encode proteins (Vittoria & Robinson, 2000). Thus, brain function and behavioral patterns can be ultimately linked to biological processes within the body and gene expression. The brain is presently not fully understood by neurobiologists and neuroanatomists, so scientists cannot definitively state whether or not one's sexual orientation can be linked to one's brain structure. There are presently theoretical difficulties and research design difficulties in the studies that have been done to date demonstrating a link between neurobiological factors in the human brain and individuals' sexual orientation. One of the underlying factors that plague research on the brain and homosexuality is that the brain is a malleable organ, and it changes throughout people's lifetimes from periods of initial development into adulthood. There are several process that influence brain structure and function, and neurobiological studies have shown that mature central nervous systems retain the ability to change through circulating hormones. Therefore, connections between neurons in the brain and the efficiency of the transmission of information throughout it can reflect interactions between developmental experiences and hormone actions. Most neurological studies claiming a difference in brains between males and females have only exposed a point in time in individuals' lives, and they do not adequately express the dynamic nature and potential plasticity of the brain.

It is unclear after decades of research whether or not the neurobiological analyses of complex behavior is even possible because it is nearly impossible to define the set of parameters adequately to sample given populations (Vittoria & Robinson, 2000). In regards to individuals' sexual orientations, people do not necessarily have to engage in heterosexual or homosexual acts to be labeled as such because it may not be adaptive and avoided because of social pressures and psychological conflict. There is also potential for individuals to have heterosexual and homosexual erotic fantasies, but they consciously or subconsciously repress them as a result of social pressures and psychological conflict. In research on homosexual individuals, there is always potential for false reporting in control groups as a result of stigmas surrounding homosexuality, and many do not take into account cross-cultural research in which individuals have heterosexual nuclear families but practice homosexuality with partners. Female sexuality has been found to be more complicated in comparison to men, and researchers have found that there is a complex relationship between women's sexual desires, orientations, and identities. Women's sexual orientations have been found to be unstable across the course of their lifetimes, and it is clear that past comparative studies establishing neat boundaries on women's sexual orientations are oversimplifications.

Future neurobiological studies on individuals' sexual orientation should be based on brain function and physiology, and they should take into consideration the complex interactions that human brains have with environments (Vittoria & Robinson, 2000). It is likely that multiple areas of the human brain are involved with sexual orientation because sexual attraction depends on multitudes of external stimuli and individual biological substrates. Biological factors and individual experiences can modify neuron connections within the brain to converge into what is ultimately one's sexual orientation, which can occur through interactive relationships between behavior and hormones or through the development specific brain structures. The use of magnetic resonance imaging, computerized axial tomography, and positron emission tomography will be instrumental in helping to define the brain areas involved in individuals' sexual orientation. The challenge for researchers will be to determine how different behavior patterns are linked to chemical and biological processes, but there are presently limitations to this type of investigation because current resolution levels of medical scanning equipment do not permit the analysis of individual groups of neurons.

Chapter 9: Homosexuality and Intelligence

The origin of individuals preferences and values is an unresolved theoretical problem in behavioral sciences, and the Savanna-Intelligent Quotient Hypothesis states that more intelligent individuals are likely to acquire and adopt preferences and values that are considered by behavioral scientists to be evolutionarily novel (Kanazawa, 2012). Anthropological studies of traditional societies have suggested that homosexual behavior was most likely rare in ancestral environments, so it is more likely that intelligent people engaged in homosexual behavior according to the Savanna-IQ Interaction Hypothesis. Evolutionary psychologists have proposed that the human brain was designed and has adapted to environments like all organs since our ancestors were walking on the African savanna during the Pleistocene Epoch. Many evolutionary psychologists believe that the evolution of general intelligence resulted from domain-specific adaptation to solve novel problems, and the logical conclusion if one agrees with the theory regarding domain-specific adaptation is that more intelligent individuals would have less difficulty adapting to novel stimuli in evolutionary unfamiliar environments than less intelligent individuals. Part of these evolutionary novel stimuli would include ideas and lifestyles that form the basis of individuals' preferences and values.

Studies have shown that more intelligent children have an increased likelihood of adopting liberal political views, which can be considered evolutionarily novel because of genuine concerns of individuals that are genetically unrelated to them and of a willingness to contribute private resources for others welfare (Kanazawa, 2012). The effect of childhood intelligence on liberal political views in adulthood is twice as large as that of sex or race. Studies have also shown that more intelligent boys have an increased likelihood to value sexual exclusivity, which is considered to be evolutionarily novel for men because throughout evolutionary history they have been naturally polygamous. This has not been the case for women throughout evolutionary history because they are expected to be sexually exclusive with a single mate in either a monogynous or polygynous marriage. Studies have shown that intelligent children are more likely to grow up to be nocturnal and some researchers believe that nightlife may be evolutionarily novel because our ancestor did not have artificial lighting, so it is accepted that our ancestors woke shortly before dawn and slept shortly after dusk in a similar manner to contemporary hunter-gatherer societies. More intelligent children have also shown to consume more legal and illegal narcotics, and it is believed that ingesting psychoactive substances is evolutionary novel because it originated less than 10,000 years ago. Finally, criminals have lower than average intelligence in comparison to the general population because murder, assault, and robbery are considered to by researchers to be a routine means of intrasexual competition for resources and mates in human ancestral environments. The institutions, however, that are used to detect and punish criminals are considered to be evolutionary novel. The behaviors engaged in by other species would be classified as criminal if engaged in by humans, and there was little justice given to criminals in the human ancestral environments with the exception of retaliation and ostracism. Therefore, individuals with lower intelligence are more like to resort to evolutionary familiar means of competition for resources and mating opportunities, and they may not fully comprehend the consequences of their behavior imposed on them by law enforcement.

Most evolutionary psychologists and biologists believe that humans have not undergone a dramatic evolutionary change over the last 10,000 years or since the end of the Pleistocene

Epoch (Kanazawa, 2012). This is the underlying assumption behind the Savanna-IQ Interaction Hypothesis, which has held up under scrutinization by some evolutionary psychologists and biologist who have argued that new alleles have emerged in the human genome during the Holocene Epoch. The implications, however, are unclear because the relevance of these new alleles is not immediately obvious, and with the exception of lactose tolerance it is not clear whether or not these new alleles have led to the emergence of new physical or psychological adaptations over the last 10,000 years. For males, individuals' sexual orientations have been shown to be scientifically determined prenatally by either genetic or prenatal hormone factors, so it is more likely that more intelligent individuals will be "truly homosexual". It is possible that genetic research in the future will uncover a link between genes for homosexuality and intelligence, and it is possible that more intelligent individuals appear to be homosexual because of the malleability of self-presentation, which would be especially true if homosexuality is evolutionary novel. Regardless of individuals "true" sexual orientations, more intelligent individuals are more likely to identify themselves as being homosexual, engage in homosexual behaviors, and report homosexual desires.

Although contemporary hunter-gatherer societies throughout the world do not live in the same environment as our ancestors, they do offer the best modern day example available for making inferences through examination of ancestral life (Kanazawa, 2012). In an examination of homosexuality currently practiced in modern hunter-gatherer tribes, the behavior is currently practiced mainly by tribes in Papua New Guinea, and it is used as part of initiation rites for boys and is culturally mandated. The homosexuality that occurs in these cultures begins in adolescence and continues into adulthood until a male is married, but it differs significantly from homosexuality by choice because the behavior is used for initiation and involves little emotional attachment. In other literature documenting hunter-gatherer tribes in both South America and Africa, occurrences of homosexuality are rare, and instances of homosexuality by ethnographers studying tribes within these regions documents four types of infrequent homosexuality that occur: mentorship, pathecism, hemophilia, and youthful experimentation. The hemophilia relationships that occur in hunter-gatherer societies are the most closely related to those of relationships of individuals who are homosexual, but there occurrence in current hunter-gatherer tribes throughout the world is rare. Examples of homosexuality depicted in cave art throughout the world are nearly non-existent, and instances found depicting homosexual acts are ambiguous and clearly open to interpretation. From the anthropological evidence of modern day hunter-gatherer tribes and cave art throughout the world, it is clear that homosexual behavior in human ancestral environments was infrequent.

Instances of homosexuality may not always be detected by ethnographers doing field work, so the absence of homosexuality by observation is not necessarily conclusive evidence that the behavior does not exist in traditional societies throughout the world (Kanazawa, 2012). Ethnographers in the field have been able to recover evidence of other behaviors that were not culturally permissible, such as: adultery, infanticide, and homicide. Therefore, the lack of documentation of homosexual behavior as a result of free choice suggests that it is rare in contemporary hunter-gatherer societies throughout the world. Thus, it can be concluded that homosexual behavior in human ancestral environments was not common, and that the behavior can be considered to be evolutionarily novel. Forms of homosexuality have been observed in many species despite exclusive homosexuality being rare in nature, but the basic biological design for all species is for heterosexual reproduction. Ethnographers' observations of traditional societies throughout the world suggest that homosexual behavior that has been witnessed has been done concurrently with heterosexual behavior. Humans are not descended from ancestors that were exclusively homosexual, so it can be inferred that homosexual behavior has not been a part of human nature throughout our evolutionary history. Some ethnographers and evolutionary psychologists disagree and believe that homosexual behavior could have possibly formed same-sex coalitions, which aided in our ancestors survival. The argument that homosexuality is evolutionary novel is also inconsistent with the argument that homophobia is evolutionarily novel and evolved as a novel psychological mechanism for dealing with homosexual behavior in environments.

In testing the hypothesis that homosexual identity and homosexual behavior are evolutionary novel and that more intelligent individuals are more likely to identify themselves as being homosexual, three large studies on homosexuality from the United States and the United Kingdom converge to support it (Kanazawa, 2012). First, childhood intelligence has been shown to be positively associated with adult homosexual identities and attraction, and more intelligent children are more likely to identify themselves as being homosexual and express homosexual attraction. Second, more intelligent individuals have been shown to have more homosexual partners in their lifetimes than less intelligent people. This association has also been found in research involving heterosexual individuals, but it is found to occur at rates of 50% or more among homosexuals in comparison to heterosexuals. More intelligent children have also been shown to have more same-sex cohabitation partners than less intelligent partners throughout their lifetimes but do not have more opposite-sex cohabitation partners over the course of their lifetimes.

There are limitations to the findings between intelligence and homosexuality (Kanazawa, 2012). The data associated with a lifetime number of homosexual partners and intelligence can also be associated with heterosexual partners and intelligence. Childhood intelligence is also not associated with expressed homosexual attraction among men, and childhood intelligence has not been found to be associated with the lifetime number of homosexual cohabitation partners among women. All of the studies used in testing these theories have small samples as a result of homosexuality being relatively rare among general populations, and among the homosexuals sampled there were low incidences of the items measured. In instances in which there was support for the theory, the size of the association was small. The research, however, does show that more intelligent men and women are more likely to adopt evolutionarily novel preferences and values than less intelligent men and women. There are many factors that influence an individual's inclination to engage in homosexual behavior, but it is clear that general intelligence is one of them. Social and cultural factors clearly influence homosexual behavior for more intelligent individuals of both sexes, and it may influence why these individuals are more likely to engage in homosexual behavior. It is likely that there is no single factor that can explain the effects of the findings regarding the sexual interaction effects of more intelligent individuals.

Pheromones

Animal studies have shown that the choice of sexual partners is influenced by pheromone signals, which are processed by males and females in the anterior hypothalamus (Savic et. al, 2005). Pheromone signals are transferred to the hypothalamus from the vomeronasal organ through the olfactory nerve. Pheromones effects on humans have been questioned because our vomeronasal pit lacks a direct neuronal connection to our brains, but scientific research suggests that this type of chemical communication cannot be ruled out for humans. Sex-steroid compounds, like androstadienone and estratetraenol, have been shown to induce gender-specific effects on human's nervous systems, moods, and levels sexual arousal. The effects of sex steroid compounds vary with the amount of steroid administered and experimental design, but they have shown to be differentiated in accordance with participants gender, especially androstadienone. Androstadienone is a derivative of testosterone and is produced primarily in male sweat, and estratetraenol resembles estrogen and is primarily detected in the urine of pregnant women. Research using the positron emission tomography and functional magnetic resonance imaging have shown that smelling both androstadienone and estratetraenol leads to brain activation. Also, male sweat has been shown to alter the luteinic hormone from the hypothalamus in females. Although androstadienone and estratetraenol cannot be presently classified as pheromones, the present scientific data suggests that they do function as at least chemosignals.

In heterosexual subjects, androstadienone and estratetraenol have been shown to cause sex-differentiated activation of the anterior hypothalamus under PET and fMRI observation (Savic et. al, 2005). Estratetraenol activation involved the paraventricular and dorsomedial nuclei in men, and androstadienone activated the preoptic area and ventromedial nuclei in women. In contrast, androstadienone in men and estratetraenol in women were found only to activate the amygdale plus piriform cortex, anterior insular cortex, orbitofrontal cortex, and anterior cingulated cortex, which are areas that have been reported to process common odors. The two steroid compounds are believed to act bimodally as both pheromones and odors, and the anterior hypothalamus primarily processes the signals of the pheromone components and the olfactory brain processes the signals of the odor components. Depending on the sexual orientation of an individual, one pathway will become dominant, and the other will become suppressed.

Preferred hypothalamic pathways are dependent on one's sexual orientation and not their sex, and sex steroids act bimodally using different pathways depending on one's sexual orientation (Savic et. al, 2005). The activation of androstadienone and estratetraenol has been shown to be clearly separable depending on individuals' gender and sexual orientation, and they clearly differed from activations caused by common odors. Androstadienone was shown to activate the hypothalamus in homosexual men and heterosexual women, but it did not have the same effect in heterosexual men (NewsRx, 2005). Heterosexual men, however, showed the same activation in the hypothalamus to estratetraenol that both homosexual men and heterosexual women showed to androstadienone. Homosexual men, heterosexual women, and heterosexual men were all found to respond similarly to common odors, which activated only the regions of the human brain involved in processing odors. The findings regarding androstadienone and estratetraenol indicate that the human brain reacts differently to sex steroids and common odors, which suggest that there is a link between individuals' sexual orientation and brain function.

Researchers have shown that male homosexuals' brains react to hormones similarly to heterosexual women, and female homosexuals brains react to hormones similarly to those of heterosexual men (Schmid, 2006). Although the similarity is not exact, it is clear that male and female homosexuals' brains react differently to hormones than male and female heterosexuals' brains. These findings support the idea that homosexuality has a genetic basis, and that it is not a learned behavior. This research supports a biological basis for homosexuality, and it should open up researchers to the possibility that there are genetic factors that contribute to individuals' sexual orientation. Androstadienone and estratetraenol are sex hormones, but they are thought to act as human pheromones, which trigger defensive and sexual behavioral responses in many animals. Research done in 2000 reported locating a gene believed to direct human pheromones to the nose, but the issue of whether humans responded to pheromones similar to other animals is not accepted to date by all biologists.

Chapter 10: Medicalization and Homosexuality

There are only a few documented examples of demedicalization of medical issues, and homosexuality is one of them (Conrad & Angell, 2004). Over the last thirty years, homosexuality has been demedicalized by the American Psychological Association as a result of areas of research, but the potential for remedicalization does exist. The roots of the medicalization can be found in the criminalization of homosexual acts in the nineteenth century, and it was believed by most physicians during this period that homosexuality resulted as a congenital disease caused by weakness in individuals nervous systems. Homosexual individuals were believed to not be able to change the direction of their sexual desires, and it was believed that the perceived disease could be resolved therapeutically. Although these medical theories were in response to the criminalization inflicted upon homosexual acts, oppressive medical treatments and psychiatric attempts to change homosexuals into heterosexuals still emerged during this period. Sigmund Freud revolutionized the way psychologists and the medical community viewed homosexuality despite being opposed to homosexual acts, and he theorized that homosexual desires were a part of normal psychological development, which needed to be abandoned and repressed in adulthood. Freud linked homosexuality to normal sexual development, and he helped to show that homosexuality was a variation and not a disease.

Psychologists that followed variations of Freud's psychodynamic theory of homosexuality reestablished homosexuality as a pathology in the mid-twentieth century (Conrad & Angell, 2004). Theories regarding homosexuality during this period led to the medicalization of homosexuality, and it was categorized it as a sexual perversion influenced by flawed childhood relationships and resulted in pathology. For psychologists in the mid-twentieth century, homosexuality was a form of mental illness that could be resolved with psychoanalytic treatments that attempted to convert homosexuals successfully into heterosexuals. In the 1968 edition of the "Diagnostic Statistical Manual of Mental Disorders", homosexuality was clearly defined as a medical pathology, and it was classified as a sexual deviation under personality disorders. During this same period, a gay social movement began in the United States that demanded an end to gay persecution and discrimination. This movement sought to present homosexuality as a healthy and normal practice and to contradict official medical views of homosexuality with psychiatric opponents, which resulted in convincing the American Psychological Association to change the classification of the homosexuality in the "Diagnostic Statistical Manual of Mental Disorders". By 1980, homosexuality was officially demedicalized, and it was no longer considered a mental illness by the American Psychological Association.

There are four areas that have influenced the medical definitions and treatment of homosexuals since the Gay Rights Movement began: psychiatry, human immunodeficiency virus and acquired immunodeficiency syndrome, genetics, and social perceptions of the gay community (Conrad & Angell, 2004). In the last three decades, there have been important changes in the field of psychology that have dramatically affected psychologists' perceptions of homosexuality, which ultimately caused an end to the medicalization of homosexuality. The psychoanalytic approach was overtaken by biomedical psychological approach, which resulted in decisions regarding the medicalization becoming increasingly based on scientific evidence and not theory. The remedicalization of homosexuality is possible, and activists within the field of psychology are presently attempting to get homosexuality classified as a gender identity disorder. For homosexuals that feel conflicted about their homosexuality, a comprised diagnosis called egodystonic homosexuality has remained a pathology despite demedicalization of homosexuality, but the emphasis is on conflict surrounding one's sexual orientation and not the inability to achieve heterosexual arousal. Egodystonic homosexuality was demedicalized in the 1980s following gay lobbying because the diagnosis continued to pathologize homosexuality.

Despite the demedicalization of homosexuality and egodystonic homosexuality, a small group of psychologists has continued to offer medical treatments for homosexuality (Conrad & Angell, 2004). These therapies offer reparative and conversion therapy to homosexuals based on the belief that homosexuality results from an unhealthy childhood development and not based on biological factors. Organizations like the National Association for Research and Therapy of Homosexuals have presently formed alliances with conservative family and religious organizations to promote their theories surrounding the curability of homosexuality. NARTH is currently attempting to get homosexuality remedicalized as a gender identity disorder, which was a classification of pathology listed in the "Diagnostic Statistical Manual of Mental Disorders" to treat transgender adults and children that exhibit cross-gender behavior. Opponents to the gender identity disorder feel the diagnosis further medicalizes homosexuality because the majority of children diagnosed with the disorder grow up to become homosexual or bisexual, so it is believed to be a normal part of development for homosexual individuals. Of boys diagnosed with gender identity disorder, 75% grow up to have homosexual and bisexual desires, but the majority of homosexuals are never diagnosed with gender identity disorder in childhood. Although gender identity disorder has been changed in the newest edition of the "Diagnostic Statistical Manual of Mental Disorders" to gender dysphoria, it is clear that the potential for remedicalizing homosexuality will always exist despite the stigma of homosexuality being reduced through gay activism because the capacity to medicalize non-mainstream behavior will always exist (Beredjick, 2012). Many individuals the gay community felt homosexuality would be remedicalized during the acquired immunodeficiency syndrome epidemic in the late twentieth century.

In the early 1980s, AIDS emerged as a deadly illness among homosexual men, and by the early 1990s it had transformed the gay community (Conrad & Angell, 2004). During this period, homosexual men were disproportionately suffering the effects of the disease, which led to gay community becoming the center of activism and research for the disease. Many sociologists feel that AIDS remedicalized homosexuality because homosexual men were some of the first to contract the disease, so being homosexual in the public's eye became a symptom of AIDS. The initial name given for the disease was gay-related immune disorder because there was a close association with the disease and homosexual lifestyles. The medical community in the early 1970s perceived homosexuality as problematic because little was understood about the disease, so this led to increased attention to the homosexual connections to the disease despite evidence of non-homosexual portions of the population contracting the disease. The medical community initially believed that the immune deficiency resulted from an immune overload as a result of homosexual lifestyles, but when it was discovered that the disease was spread through viral transmission focus shifted away from homosexuals, and attention was given to lifestyle choices that could lead to the transmission of the disease. Homosexuals' behavior was medicalized to a point during the initial discovery of AIDS, and the media in conjunction with the religious right continued to portray AIDS as a "gay disease".

The discovery of AIDS led to increased stigmatization of homosexuality, and fear of the disease led increased fear of homosexuality and the immorality of the lifestyles (Conrad & Angell, 2004). This led to discrimination against homosexuals seeking employment, medical care, and education, which was enhanced by fears of contracting the disease. The perceived connection between AIDS and homosexuality led to medical neglect of diseased patients and monitoring of homosexuals behavior. The association between AIDS and homosexuality led to the closure of bathhouses, concerns surrounding the donation of blood by homosexuals, and debate regarding mandatory testing. As a result of a lack of government funding for research, the disease remained misunderstood for nearly a decade, which resulted in the deaths and infections of countless numbers of individuals. Medical surveillance of homosexuals renewed stigmatizations against the behavior, but it did not remedicalize homosexuality. This was a result of gay activism towards the disease and the societal reactions to it. Activists exposed the neglect, pushed for continued research, and provided hospice services in the early years following the discovery of the disease. The activism resulted in an increased alliance between the gay community and physicians, which resulted in increased gay-friendly sexual guidelines and increased dialogue about common gay sexual practices.

Genetic connections were not commonly hypothesized by research throughout most of the twentieth century until the 1990s because of the lack of credible research that had been presented to the public in the first half of the century regarding eugenics and the horrors experienced during World War II with the Holocaust (Conrad & Angell, 2004). During the 1990s, there was an upsurge in research connecting genetics and homosexuality as a result of the cultural climate and the Human Genome Project, which established an increased openness to genetic explanations of behavior. The research linking genetics and homosexuality in the early 1990s associated the behavior with smaller hypothalami, increased rates of homosexuality between identical twins, and a linkage between deoxyribonucleic acid on X chromosomes and male sexual orientations. The studies were well received by the public and had extensive media coverage, and they also scientifically established a link between biophysiology and genetics to homosexual behavior. Despite some of the studies lacking ability to be replicated, the term "gay gene" was coined by the popular media. This is a great concern for the gay community because it is believed that it could lead to genetic testing for the behavior, which ultimately could result in the remedicalization of homosexuality.

The results of the renewed interest between genetics and behavior caused the gay community to embrace their sexual orientation in the 1990s with the majority of homosexuals believing that there is a biological explanation for their same-sex preferences (Conrad & Angell, 2004). The biological explanation for homosexuality became popular in the gay community because it fit with the current rhetoric of homosexual politics, and this allowed homosexuals' attorneys to argue for their civil rights because the condition was scientifically considered permanent and it also countered the beliefs of the religious right who considered the behavior a psychopathology. The affirmation of the "gay gene" by the gay community has changed the manner in which the medical establishment understands and treats homosexuals, and this has resulted in the United States Department of Health and Human Services to include sexual orientation as an important demographic for biomedical research and health concerns.

The general trend in medicine over the last century has been toward medicalizing human problems, but there are a small number of cases that have resulted in nearly complete demedicalization, which includes homosexuality (Conrad & Angell, 2004). Issues in the following areas could potentially lead to the remedicalization of homosexuality: psychiatry, HIV/AIDS, genetics, and social perceptions of the gay community. Since the beginning of the demedicalization of homosexuality in the 1970s, there have been contested areas of the transformation of the medical community's view on the behavior, but for the most part the demedicalization of homosexuality has endured for nearly five decades. The changes seen in the field of psychiatry have been mixed, and views regarding childhood gender deviance will continue to potentially remedicalize homosexuality in the future. During the 1980s, it appeared that treatment of HIV/AIDS would potentially lead to the remedicalization of homosexuality, but it has not presently contributed to the remedicalization of homosexuality despite the increased social stigmatization toward homosexuals. With renewed interest in genetics over the last three decades, there has been growing support in the gay community for genetic "gay gene" investigation, and hope that homosexuality will be viewed as a sexual orientation rather than a sexual preference. The gay community is divided on its position toward genetic hypotheses regarding homosexuality because some individuals believe it could ultimately result in genetic therapy for homosexuals while others feel it is the key to maintain demedicalization of the behavior. Arguments for the remedicalization of homosexuality have clearly shifted with from psychiatry to genetics over the last three decades, and the increased support of genetic research will most likely continue to find slight genetic differences leading to homosexuality being viewed as a biomedical disorder in the future. Despite current genetic data being contested and limited, the power of the genetic perspective can be seen in its public support and the publicity new findings receive. It is clear that it is not the genetic findings that are significant for maintaining the demedicalization of homosexuality but how they are interpreted by the scientific community and the public. Forty years following the American Psychological Association's demedicalization of homosexuality, the behavior remains subject to social stigmas, but it is not likely that remedicalization of it will occur.

Chapter 11: Male Homosexual Body Image

The concept of ideal male body and masculinity differs between heterosexual and homosexual men, and both have become shaped differently as a result of the media's portrayal of their ideal images (Glaser, 2006). Homosexual men have been shaped by mass media as being weak and broken individuals, which have been sharply contrasted by the media's depiction of heterosexual males as being strong and healthy individuals. Following the Gay Rights Movement in the 1970s, increased levels of social tolerance began to result as media attention increased the visibility of homosexual men in high social positions, and discourse on homosexuality became a more frequent subject in types of entertainment. As a result of human immunodeficiency virus and acquired immunodeficiency syndrome, the improved status that resulted from the Gay Rights Movement experienced some setbacks as the link between the disease and homosexual lifestyle increasingly became represented in mass media. The connection between homosexual men and HIV/AIDS continued through the 1990s, but the decade saw the introduction of positive homosexual role models on popular television shows. The twenty-first century saw an increase in gay-specific advertising as a result of corporate markets targeting the large amount of discretionary income that homosexual men had, and it is believed that this increased exposure targeted specifically at gay men resulted in greater body image dissatisfaction despite the overall improved portrayal of homosexuality within contemporary mass media.

Homosexual male society has created its own set of norms and standards like all individuated communities, and this has resulted in the homosexual male community creating a unique set of ideals surrounding body image, which are characterized by aesthetic norms reflected in all-male idolization of young, muscular, and smooth physiques (Glaser, 2006). Homosexual males achieve their ideal body in a similar fashion to heterosexual males, but the techniques differ in that they are driven by an attempt to overcome the heteronormative oppression produced by images from the gay media and reinforced socially within the gay community. Ideal images within the gay community include young men who are slim or muscular, and the result is the exclusion of other non-ideal body types within the gay community. Within the gay community, there are categories used to identify and distinguish its members: effeminate, muscular and macho, hairy sadomasochistic bear, and the boyish twink. As a result of these labels, the homosexual community has become increasingly segregated, and the need to categorize these members has resulted in increased social pressure on homosexual men.

Male Homosexual Body Image Dissatisfaction

Research has suggested that homosexual men have a high risk for body image dissatisfaction, which contributes to their perceived acceptance as members of the gay community, their social comparison tendencies, levels of body image satisfaction, self-esteem, and rates of depression (Levesque & Vichesky, 2006). Homosexual men have increased concerns regarding muscularity in comparison to heterosexual men, and there is strong evidence that body-image and self-esteem are moderately integrated within the gay community, which contributes to members level of involvement and perceptions of acceptance. In the history of body image research, the majority of it has focused on females, and they comprise approximately 90% of individuals diagnosed with eating disorders. Caucasian women have expressed increased body dissatisfaction in comparison to men, and women in general express a desire to be thinner and often believe they weigh more than they do. Numerous research studies on women's body dissatisfaction has attributed it to exposure of images of ideal body types shown within the media, which results in self-comparison and internalized dissatisfaction that causes increased rates of low self-esteem, depression, and eating disorders.

Although the research on men's perceptions of their body images has not been as common as research on women's perceptions of their body images, evidence has shown that more than 40% are dissatisfied with their body images and their general appearance (Levesque & Vichesky, 2006). The underlying nature of men's dissatisfaction differs from women, and research has shown that men desire to be thinner and more muscular as opposed to just thinner. Typically, younger and underweight males have a desire to be more muscular, and groups of older men have shown desire to reduce their weight. Men who experience body dissatisfaction experience a variety of negative consequences as a result: low self-esteem, engagement in risky eating behaviors, and steroid abuse. Research on men's perceptions of their body images has shown that their dissatisfaction can result in poor psychological and physical health. Concern over body images are more pronounced in homosexual men in comparison to heterosexual men, and research on men with disorders resulting from a dissatisfaction with body image has shown that homosexual men are at a greater risk for developing eating disorders than heterosexual men.

Research studies have shown that homosexual men are divided in their unhappiness regarding their body images (Levesque & Vichesky, 2006). Some gay men's ideal body physique is underweight while others desire muscularity, and it is believed that the exhibited strong drive for muscularity is because of an association with it and masculinity. Within the gay community, muscularity has become a symbol of health over the last four decades as it has dealt with the impact of HIV/AIDS. Researchers have interpreted aspects of gay male culture to support the disproportionate number of homosexuals at risk for body dissatisfaction, and there are several studies that have suggested that male homosexual culture emphasizes physical appearance more than heterosexual male culture, which is attributed to the need to attract other men and a tendency for homosexual men to attribute physical appearance strongly with self-concepts. Therefore, researchers believe that homosexual men with body dissatisfaction may undergo powerful psychological processes regarding their self-esteem, which can potentially lead to serious depression. Research studies have shown that a significant predictor of male homosexuals' body dissatisfaction is their level participation within the gay community, and it has been found that one's increased involvement within the gay community leads to increased body dissatisfaction. It is believed as homosexual men become more integrated into the culture that they are more frequently exposed to ideal body types and experience pressure to conform to them. Researchers believe that social comparisons within the gay community are heavily influenced by dominate media images of men, and as a result of media promotion of ideal men becoming increasingly muscular homosexual men may have heightened body dissatisfaction concerns in respect to their muscularity.

Recent studies have confirmed associations between homosexual men's body satisfaction and self-esteem, and that body image concerns are important to homosexual men's psychological well-being (Levesque & Vichesky, 2006). Preoccupation with one's weight has been correlated with levels of depression in homosexual men, and homosexual men's body image satisfaction appears to be important because of its relationship to self-esteem. As homosexual men become increasingly integrated within gay culture, the level of body image satisfaction as it correlates to individuals' self-esteem declines as a result of perceived acceptance within the gay community, so the relationship between body image and self-esteem can only be applied to homosexual men who have low or moderate integration within the gay community.

Body Image and Homosexual Women

Psychological research has related individuals' body image satisfaction to increased rates of dieting, anorexia nervosa, and bulimia nervosa (Herzog et al., 1992). Rates of eating disorders for homosexual women have been shown to be consistently lower than heterosexual women, which shows that they have more satisfaction with their bodies. Women, however, as a whole generally desire to weigh less than their ideal body weight, but this clearly does not define how society views women's body shapes, which suggests that a more accurate measurement for ideal body weight and physiques for women should be through the social pressures imposed upon them through males' perceptions of ideal female physiques. Of the few studies that have been conducted on the relationship between women's sexual orientation and body satisfaction, it was reported that homosexual women are less concerned with physical appearance than heterosexual women, and homosexual women who were sexually involved with other women felt more body satisfaction than women who were not.

There are similarities between heterosexual and homosexual women who have both been shown to be statistically concerned with their weight, and 40% women in one research study felt they were overweight despite being at or below their correct weight in relation to tables used by national insurance companies (Herzog et al., 1992). Both heterosexual and homosexual women believed that they weighed more than the weight that potential partners would find attractive or an ideal weight for attractiveness. In comparison of heterosexual and homosexual women, heterosexual women have shown to be more concerned with weight and appearance than homosexual women despite their similarities. Heterosexual women show more body dissatisfaction than homosexual women and were more likely to be underweight. For women who were at a normal weight, homosexual women have shown to be more satisfied with their bodies than heterosexual women and expressed less concern about needing to lose weight than heterosexual women. These findings clearly show that homosexual women are more satisfied with their bodies than homosexual women and should be at less of a risk for body image dissatisfaction and at risk for eating disorders, and that homosexual women have a different standard for ideal body weight and physiques than heterosexual women.

Psychosocial approaches to understanding the differences between heterosexual and homosexual women's perceptions of body image suggest that it may result from homosexual women being more interpersonally oriented and less independent than heterosexual women (Herzog et al., 1992). All women internalize and endorse cultural norms, and it is believed by most psychologists that individuals sex roles are connected to the media's portrayal of ideal images. Typically, the media's portrayal of successful, independent, and high-achieving women is thin, which is believed to be a contributing factor for susceptibility to eating disorders. Research on girls has shown that female children who strive to be independent, thin, and successful have an increased susceptibility to eating disorders because of an underlying association between thinness and success. Despite all girls being concerned with appearance, girls who desired a female appearance that was nurturing and caring were shown to not be as prone to eating disorders. Homosexual women have been shown through social science research to be more nurturing and interpersonally oriented than heterosexual women who typically display more autonomy and independence. Female homosexual ideology typically rejects contemporary societal standards of female beauty and allows homosexual women to nurture themselves to overcome the guilt associated with not being "ideal".

Since homosexual relationships promote satisfaction and acceptance of one's body, homosexual women have a decreased risk of developing eating disorders in comparison to heterosexual women (Herzog et al., 1992). Homosexual women prefer being heavier, are more satisfied with their physiques, and are less concerned with appearance than heterosexual women. These attitudes sharply contrast the powerful drive for thinness that pervade beliefs within the heterosexual female population regarding "ideal" body types, and it explains the lower rate of eating disorders found among homosexual women in comparison.

Chapter 12: Homosexuality and Children

Throughout the twentieth century, homosexuality was considered a mental illness, and this prevailing belief dominated much of the research done by both pediatricians and child-mental health experts (Harris, 2003). This is reflected in articles regarding pre-adolescent same-sex behavior, which focus on male pre-adolescents and cites homosexual behavior in boys as resulting from inadequate family relationships. Pre-adolescent boys who engage in behavior of the opposite sex were portrayed as developing homosexual identities, and other causes discussed included associations between boys with a need for emotional security and homosexual men.

"The manifestations of homosexuality ranged from overt practice to the adoption of behavior patterns characteristic of the other sex. In addition, there were other personality disturbances, presumably related to an inadequate home life. Feelings of inferiority and insecurity were common and expressed themselves in fears and episodes of running away... A craving for affection and reassurance was a prominent feature and was dependent on a past which was affectionless. Many, however, were unable to show affection or form lasting attachments. Aggressive behavior toward small children and submissive behavior toward older playmates were frequent." (Bawkin & Bawkin, 1953, p. 108)

During the same period, innovative research was being conducted by Dr. Evelyn Hooker on homosexual men, and there was no evidence of mental illness found with the exception of the chronic stress being endured by individuals resulting from living in a society that was non-accepting of their sexuality (Harris, 2003). This research and confirmations of her findings resulted in the change of homosexuality being classified as a pathological condition in the "Diagnostic and Statistical Manual Mental Disorders" in 1973. Over the last 50 years, our understanding of pre-adolescent behavior and homosexuality has progressed a great deal, and science has helped disprove dissimilar areas of comparison and broad generalizations formerly attributed to pre-adolescent and homosexual behavior.

Sexual Identity and Adolescence

The formation of one's sexual identity is a primary task during adolescence, and part of developing this identity is testing and confirming feelings that an individual is undergoing (Wilson, 1999). For individuals that are homosexual, this process can be problematic and result in feelings of isolation because of a lack of opportunity to meet others in similar situations. This isolation may result in unresolved sexual identity issues, which may cause some individuals to enter their actual adolescence following their chronological adolescence. The consequence of dealing with one's distinct sexual identity may lead to a referral for professional help, but the majority of gay adolescent males are able to deal psychologically with their identities. The cause of referral to psychiatrists by the majority of adolescents is usually for issues that are not directly related to their sexual identities, but the secondary psychiatric symptoms resulting from conflict with their sexual identity may result in psychiatric referrals. The majority of adolescents that are referred to psychiatrists are for depression, psychosomatic illnesses, and self-esteem issues. Adolescents suffering from sexual identity issues or secondary psychiatric symptoms may also have eating disorders and express dissatisfaction with their bodies, and increased levels of suicide have been documented by researchers in adolescents dealing with sexual identity issues.

The process of developing an identity as a homosexual involves "coming out" to family members and friends regarding one's sexual orientation, and this requires an internalized resolution of homophobia by these individuals prior to informing others of their attraction to the same-sex (Wilson, 1999). This process is complex, and it requires both intrapersonal and interpersonal transformation. The entire process begins in adolescence and extends into adulthood, and it is accompanied by developmental stages, which eventually results in an acceptance of one's sexual orientation. The various developmental stages identified serve as a framework for psychiatrists to assess individuals and intervene if necessary. There have been different theoretical models presented by psychologists regarding the stages homosexuals go through in accepting their sexual identities. Woodman and Lenna proposed the "denial" and "bargaining" stages, which separate one's initial experience in recognizing their homosexuality and their later development of a sexual identity. The bargaining or later stage may involve an individual accepting his or her sexual identity or result in an individual attempting to develop a heterosexual identity. Cass proposes that there are two stages to the development of individuals' sexual identities: personal and social. One's sexual identity is a process of integration between these two aspects of self, and individuals can commit identity foreclosure at any point in the process of merging these two aspects of self in which the process is consciously ended. Examples of this can be seen in individuals who have homosexual identities coupled with homosexual behavior, but they appear publicly as heterosexuals. The impact of embracing one's homosexual identity varies from individual to individual, and often a reluctance to embrace a homosexual identity may be the result of reasoning regarding one's individual life circumstances.

History of Homosexual Identities

The nineteenth century marked the beginning of the psychological recognition and investigation of the concept of sexual identity despite millennia of erotic thoughts, feelings, and behavior by both heterosexuals and homosexuals (Wilson, 1999). Since this period in psychological development, sexual identity has come to be considered an integrated aspect of one's overall self-identity. Societies throughout the world at the end of the twentieth century and into the twenty-first century have seen the emergence of homosexual identities, which has become known as a set of cultural beliefs, institutions, and artifacts that contribute toward modern homosexual men's and women's identity as members. Within this community, the term "homosexual" has become offensive because it represents a time when homosexuality was considered a psychopathology by the psychiatric community. Although egodystonic homosexuality was removed from the International Classification of Diseases at the end of the twentieth century, it is still considered to be a disorder by some psychologists, especially in the psychoanalytic school of thinking.

There is a great deal of confusion in the scientific community regarding the cause of homosexuality, and the implications of this have carried over into the psychiatric intervention and assessment of the behavior (Wilson, 1999). Studies that have been conducted regarding homosexual behavior have further added to the controversy surrounding the cause of homosexuality. Many of these studies have claimed links between homosexuality and child abuse, and relationships between men convicted of sexual assault and their ranges of attraction, which were from adult heterosexuals to bisexuals. Many of the studies concluding that there is a link between homosexuality and child abuse have been found to be flawed, and the distinction between male-to-male abuse and adult homosexuality was clearly not made in their design. These studies and others like it have significantly confused the public's concept of sexual orientation and its acceptance of adult homosexuality. Other research has attempted to identify biological causes behind homosexuality, which have focused on prenatal hormones and genetic influences.

Despite research and alternative theories regarding sexual orientation, homosexuality is presently still a controversial topic (Wilson, 1999). At a minimum, the entire body of research that has been done on homosexuality has allowed psychologists to recognize that individuals' sexuality is diverse and results from a complex set of factors. Psychologists working with adolescent patients suffering from secondary diseases as a result of their homosexuality must be able to identify aspects of their patient's developing sexuality, and understand how individuals' identities are affected as a result of differing circumstances. Psychologists must be aware of their own attitudes and potential homophobia in treating homosexual with secondary diseases because it can negatively impact assessments and interventions. The approach used by psychologists with homosexual patients can circumvent assumptions, and only by recognizing the unique challenges that face homosexual adolescents is it possible to provide psychological services that meet patients needs.

Homosexuality and Victimization

There have been a number of epidemiological studies on the rates of homosexual and bisexual individuals' levels of depression, suicide, substance abuse, and human immunodeficiency virus infections (Friedman et al., 2008). Adolescent and young adult homosexual men that report having sex show elevated levels for the aforementioned conditions in comparison to heterosexuals. This early onset of psychosocial and other health problems suggest that experiences of homosexuals during their adolescence influences their experiences of health problems in adulthood. Homosexual and bisexual adolescents experience increased rates of physical victimization in comparison to heterosexual control groups, and research has shown that these individuals are nine times more likely to be victimized by their peers and for longer durations. General populations of adolescents that include individuals with multiple sexual orientations who are subject to bullying have been shown to have worse health outcomes from their youth into adulthood.

The differential levels of peer victimization experience by homosexual adolescence has been attributed to the timing of individuals developmental milestones, and the age in which individuals "come out" about their sexuality has been shown to correlate with the level exposure to victimization and violence that they suffer, which has also been shown to coincide directly with the development of psychosocial problems and other health problems (Friedman et al., 2008). A compounding factor associated with the differential rates of peer victimization and associated health problems of homosexual individuals in their adolescence is that they typically have few resources to cope with victimization and violence, and this puts them at a greater risk for developing poorer health. Earlier homosexual developmental milestones led to increased experiences of abuse and worse health outcomes, which are associated with forced sex, harassment, and physical abuse prior to adulthood.

Experiences of abuse in adolescence related to one's same-sex orientation have been found to contribute to adult health problems that homosexuals experience (Friedman et al., 2008). Homosexual development cannot be entirely attributed to forced sex experiences by individuals in their adolescence, but there has been some association found between it and adult sexual orientation. Individuals who do not conform to gender roles are believed to have to confront their homosexuality at younger ages as a result of being labeled by their peers, which leads to increased victimization and poorer health at earlier ages. Some of the health problems experienced by gay and bisexual men are a result of peer victimization in adolescence, and research has shown that the level of these disparities is due in part to the milestones undergone by homosexuals in their development. Psychologists and other health professionals developing effective prevention and intervention programs for homosexual adolescents and adults must be aware of the potential of victimization experienced and the resulting discrepancy of health problems experienced between homosexuals and heterosexuals.

Homosexual men and women have reported higher numbers psychological, physical, and sexual abuse than heterosexuals (Balsam et al., 2005). Researchers have attributed victimization of homosexual men and women to others perceptions regarding homosexuality and stereotypes surrounding genders. For individuals who have shared their homosexuality with friends and family, their risk factors for substance abuse, having sex with multiple partners, and running away from home as teenagers increases as discrimination and rejection is experienced. In adulthood, homosexual men have more intimate relationships with other men than heterosexual men, so they are at a greater risk for domestic violence and sexual assault. There are a variety of factors affecting homosexual men and women in both their childhood and adulthood, which place them at psychological, physical, and sexual risk in comparison to heterosexuals.

Higher rates of physical and sexual victimization have been reported by homosexual men and women in both childhood and adulthood, and the rates reported between homosexual of both sexes and bisexuals of both sexes were found to be statistically similar, which suggests that individuals with same-sex behavior and homosexual identities are at greater risk for victimization than heterosexuals (Balsam et al., 2005). The variance in sexual orientation seen in childhood by homosexuals is attributed to the effects and higher rates of child abuse, and this information suggests that homosexuals are singled out by parents for psychological and physical maltreatment. Researchers have also found elevated rates of childhood sexual abuse in both homosexual men and women, which have been found to be greater among homosexual men than women. Bisexual men reported the highest rates of childhood sexual abuse at 45%, and homosexual men and women reported similar rates at 32%, which were significantly higher than the 12% of heterosexuals that reported childhood sexual abuse. As a result of these findings, there appears to be a direct correlation between early sexual experiences and individuals sexual attractions, behaviors, and identities.

It is clear that being homosexual increases one's risk of childhood abuse and victimization (Balsam et al., 2005). There is a correlation between homosexual behavior, social norms, and abuse. Children who become aware of same-sex attractions have little freedom in approaching others sexually in comparison to their heterosexual counterparts, and many homosexual boys will turn to men to express their sexuality. This results in increased victimization of homosexual boys because it increases their exposure to sexual abuse by adult male perpetrators. Research has shown that increased rates of sexual abuse between homosexual boys and male perpetrators, and the cycle of victimization that begins in homosexual adolescents' childhoods carries into adulthood. Homosexual men and women have reported increased rates of victimization in adulthood in comparison to heterosexuals. Investigation into homosexual adult victimization has uncovered that both homosexual men and women report increased rates of victimization by partners in relationships in comparison to heterosexuals, and homosexual men and women also reported shorter durations of relationships than heterosexual men and women. This research shows that for homosexual women lesbian relationships are not a safe from physical abuse, which sharply contrasts stereotypes surrounding lesbian relationships held by some researchers and the public. Stressors and internalized homophobia surrounding one's homosexual orientation contribute to violence in homosexual relationships, and it also increases the possibility that history of childhood victimization and the increased rates in homosexual men and women contribute to the violence in homosexual relationships.

The findings regarding sexual assault levels of homosexual men and women in adulthood show a sharp increase in comparison to heterosexuals (Balsam et al., 2005). Over 10% of homosexual and bisexual men report being raped in adulthood in comparison to less than 2% of heterosexual men. For homosexual women, the experience of rape occurs at twice the rate of that for heterosexual women, and nearly 20% of homosexual women reported that they had experienced rape during adulthood. In adulthood, one's same-sex orientation clearly increases the likelihood that they will experience victimization or rape in comparison to heterosexuals, but it is unclear what factors put homosexuals at greater risk for rape in adulthood. Since the majority of rapes occur when individuals are dating or in a relationship, homosexual individuals who partner primarily or exclusively with an individual are at a lower risk of rape. The rates of victimization for bisexual males and females have been shown to be slightly higher than those of homosexual individuals, but the exact reason for the slight increase is unknown.

Psychologists working with homosexual men and women should be aware of the increased risk of psychological, physical, and sexual victimization that could be impacting the lives of their clients (Balsam et al., 2005). Psychologists should conduct thorough assessments of their clients' victimization history and assess their current victimization risk in a manner that does not incorporate gender-based stereotypes of victims and perpetrators. Psychologists need to be aware that homosexual men experience levels of risk for sexual victimization that is more similar to heterosexual women than men. Psychologists must recognize the implications of this victimization on their clients' mental health, family relationships, and partner relationships. Most homosexual clients have experienced direct victimization or indirect victimization through their social network.

Chapter 13: Homosexual Marriage

Attitudes toward sexuality have undergone dramatic changes in all societies over the last fifty years, especially in Western societies (Kortner, 2008). One of the underlying problems facing sexual ethics is the religious acceptance of alternative lifestyles, specifically long-term relationships of same-sex couples. The debate regarding the religious acceptance of homosexual marriage is centered on whether the form of human sexuality expressed by homosexuals has equal status to heterosexuals. The social changes seen throughout the world over the past fifty years in relation to sexuality and gender confront historical sexual and social ethics with new challenges. Sexual ethics, like all questions of morality, are subject to religious interpretation and opinions, which center on the testified word of God, faith, and action. Religious texts have statuses as sources and have significant influence on individuals' formation of opinions regarding issues of morality, but experience and rationality can also be considered significant as well. Therefore, theological ethics should be considered an attempt to deal critically with the experience of life, which is guided by religious texts and enables the exercise of responsible moral decision-making within societies.

There is a distinction between legality and morality in both modern ethics and theological-ethical reflection, and both of these distinctions must be accommodated for by individuals when forming opinions regarding sexual ethics (Kortner, 2008). Conflicts of individuals surrounding sexual ethics lie within the overlap between personal theological interpretation and social ethics. From a theological perspective, many individuals are guided by religious organization's interpretations through governing bodies in relation to morally acceptable sexual practices, so questions regarding sexual ethics for many are also based on religious interpretation as it pertains to general social ethics. Religious guidance and social ethics of morality have made the interpretations of individuals' sexuality within society subject to a dramatic change, and changes in sexuality, matrimony, and family must be properly examined through ethical viewpoints and socio-historical interpretations of them.

In consideration of the history behind the interpretation of sexual ethics, it must be noted that religious interpretations of sexuality have been narrow and conservative, and these have been traditionally been imposed on matrimony, family, and work in societies throughout the world (Kortner, 2008). Presently, one of the main moral questions facing religious institutions and governing bodies is whether or not they should acknowledge long-term homosexual relationships and under what conditions. The debate regarding the equal status of homosexual partnerships is centered on the consideration of it with heterosexual relationships. To consider homosexual relationships for matrimony, one has to critically reconsider religious interpretation of heterosexual monogamy as being the only acceptable form of relationship within society, and it requires an individual not to challenge historical perspectives on matrimony and to gain a new understanding of family as it pertains to contemporary societies. Historically, religious institutions have interpreted social structures within society based on heterosexual matrimony to be naturalistic and God given, but this interpretation assumes that intact social orders are eternal and unalterable. This theological approach does not include criteria in which individuals can distinguish between those that are divinely guided and those that are not. This assumption fails to take into consideration that naturalistic order, according to the theological perspective, always appears within society, which views social orders in a manner that is unchangeable. Historically, social orders have been extremely alterable, and from a critical perspective social orders have been abused routinely in the past as a result of nationalism, racism, and political abuse. Social aspects of human life demand structures and institutions and be malleable if necessary, and as antiquated institutions disappear or change socially acceptable equivalents emerge to meet societal needs.

Ethical reflections must take into consideration freedom and fate of personhood, and all ethical actions performed by individuals are based on natural conditions (Kortner, 2008). Two aspects of biology are given: individuals' biological sex leading to potential propagation and individuals' sociality. Childhood and parenthood can be considered socially universal because individuals cannot exist without biological parents and develop without someone else's care. Family is the basic structure of human sociality because individuals are completely dependent on others in early life and at various periods throughout life. Family and sexuality can be considered symbiotic in relation to human sociality, but they must be distinguished in consideration of individuals' personal sexuality because it is an extension of an individual's personal identity. Sexuality is a form of language and can be considered a medium of personal communication, which is not innate and should be considered an aspect of an individual's disposition. Therefore, sexuality should be considered to have its own value, and an individual's sexual orientation must be respected in a similar manner to one's dignity. Matrimony is a social institution and cannot be considered a natural condition because human beings are designed for personal responsibility, and without culturally formed and morally reflected social institutions sexuality and social structures would not resemble families. Matrimony is a social institution that has been given legal value by culturally constructed social systems that are considered ethical by governing bodies, so the institution of matrimony found in nearly every society throughout the world can be considered a social institution and not a natural condition. Matrimony is such an interconnected institution with nearly every society that a society without it in some form is virtually inconceivable, but matrimony is quite diverse and varies from society to society as a result of family patterns.

The distinctiveness and concept of matrimony results from individuals living together as man and woman and parent and child, and matrimonies that end in durable partnerships include the possibility of parenthood (Kortner, 2008). Societal interest in institutionalizing marriage is not rooted in the phenomenon of love or sexuality but in progeny. Matrimony and family function as socially guiding principles because of the overlap of sexuality and the chain of generations created through the progeny they assist in facilitating. The guiding function of matrimony is the voluntariness of the act and the love that assists in creating lifelong partnerships, and marriage enables the integration of sexuality into a shared way of living, which enriches individuals' lives, helps people in times of crisis, and creates environments to raise children securely.

Interpretations of theological texts view the social institution of matrimony between man and woman as an extension of God's will, but religious texts discussion of matrimony offers little guidance for aspects of matrimony that are commonly practiced in modern day societies (Kortner, 2008). Matrimony can be interpreted as a lifelong union between a man and a woman according to theological interpretations, but it does not accommodate for divorce or culturally induced forms of matrimony within many societies. Individuals, however, can easily argue that theological texts support individuals' sex drives and personal love resulting in the institutionalization of heterosexual marriage, but it is clear that literalist interpretations of theological texts may not be social ethical in modern day society or practical.

Religious Positions on Homosexuality

Theological evaluation of homosexual lifestyles and partnerships has resulted in it being considered controversial among religious institutions, and members of these institutions remain deeply divided over issues surrounding alternative lifestyles and matrimony (Kortner, 2008). Religious institutions typically only endorse matrimony for heterosexual oriented people and couples, and contemporary theological interpretation of religious texts coupled with historical interpretations has only accepted homosexual lifestyles for individuals who are abstaining from homosexual acts and living. Religious institutions have not acknowledged homosexual forms of living in which individuals experience happiness and durable relationships, which are similar to heterosexual relationships in that they are monogamous and have all the same obligations to socially accepted forms of matrimony. The irony of religious institutions position on homosexual marriage is that the acceptance of alternative matrimonies would not result in the function of marriage acting as a guide for families and guiding principles of morality, and it could arguably strengthen the social principles that are presently endorsed by religious institutions in relation to matrimony. Alternative lifelong relationships, like homosexual matrimony, can acquire social functions that are desirable and beneficial to society, which could result in stabilizing the identities and personalities of individuals that have same-sex sexual orientations

Blessings offered by religious institutions for matrimony are not for individuals but for couples, and this represents a couple's formal expression of a joint effort to develop their relationship within an institutional scope by relying on God (Kortner, 2008). By blessing a relationship through matrimony in a religious institution, the ceremony expresses the individuals and the religious communities' devotion toward God and endorsement of social practices that are beneficial for individuals' lives. According to contemporary theological interpretation, matrimony within a religious institution is only justifiable if it is in accordance to the word of God, which is represented in numerous religious texts and dependent upon individuals' religious beliefs. God's blessing can also rest on socially alternative forms of lifelong partnerships, whether they are endorsed within a society or not, because they benefit the individuals within partnerships and environments in which they are practiced. One crucial criterion for both religious and social support for alternative matrimonies is that they be holistic and indefinitely formed relationships involving legal commitments underlying the unions similar to those of heterosexual marriages. The division of religious authorities' acceptance of homosexual lifestyles has resulted in the acceptance of homosexual matrimonies under private authorities, which should be considered problematic because it undermines the notion of blessing relationships. Privately blessing homosexual relationships and publicly denouncing homosexual lifestyles has effectively compromised the nature of blessings, especially public blessings. This has functioned to divide religious authorities and the connectedness of church services, which has effectively excluded religious members who have expressed their will to live in lifelong relationships in a responsible manner through God's grace and mercy.

Homosexuality and Freedom

There are strict rules within society governing acceptable forms of marriages, and many individuals in nations throughout the world view the legal acceptance of homosexual marriage as a struggle against injustice and discrimination (Bernheim, 2013). Both heterosexuals and homosexuals alike are asked to accept alternative forms of matrimonies by being open-minded in the name of equality despite it challenging the foundations of societies. Unfortunately, individuals often neglect to consider that just because a couple loves each other it does not necessarily grant them the right to be married, and marriage is not necessarily possible for all individuals who seek to have their love recognized legally. Restrictions would still exist on unions between individuals who are related and individuals seeking to marry multiple partners at the same time. Marriage has historically been the recognition between a loving man and woman, which makes possible parent-child relationships and organizes the lives of communities' members. Other contemporary views of marriages see them as obsolete and representing the rigidity of past institutions. The acceptance of homosexual marriage within society replaces the historic institution of marriage into a legal category that is sexless, and it results in undermining the foundations of individuals and families.

Many in favor of homosexual marriage falsely believe that permitting it will offer homosexual partners protection after the loss of a spouse, but marriage as a civil union does not automatically guarantee the protection of partners of homosexual couples (Bernheim, 2013). This protection only occurs when a marriage is legally contracted, and the protection afforded to homosexual couples under civil unions is completely dependent on the economic and legal parameters of the nation in which they are permitted to do so. In many nations, a partner in civil unions cannot inherit similarly to a spouse that has been legally married, and the taxation that follows inheritance of a civil union can be similar to that of an individual who is drawn up as a designated heir of a will.

Those who favor homosexual marriage incorrectly believe that the love of homosexual couples can provide children the same structure that is necessary for rearing that is offered by heterosexual couples (Bernheim, 2013). There is little doubt in the minds of logical individuals on both sides of the argument surrounding homosexual, and homosexuals can undoubtedly offer love to children in a similar manner to heterosexual couples. The role of parenting extends beyond the love of individuals to children, and it must be noted that a parent-child bond is fundamentally important to children's psychological development and sense of identity. All the love in the world from a homosexual couple is not sufficient to meet and produce the basic psychological structures necessary to meet a child's needs. Children's identities are established through differentiation, and this presupposes that a child knows whom he or she resembles. It is critical for children to know the differences in the love and affection displayed from men and women, which can subsequently only be found in heterosexual relationships. The sexual differences of parents represent a clear and coherent genealogy for children, which is necessary for developing their identities as individuals. Children's parentage is immensely important in serving as adult references for their own identities, and it also situates a generational chain in which children are guaranteed individual places in the world. The acceptance of homosexual marriage creates the possibility of irreversibly scrambling generational chains of identity that are necessary, which potentially risks the healthy development of children's identities and puts the foundations of society at risk. The foundation of marriage has not been based on sexuality of individuals but on sex itself, and the anthropological distinction between man and woman is necessary to create lines of paternity and maternity necessary for proper development. The reality is that under most nations homosexual parenting already exists because laws already allow for the reorganization of families permitting the sharing of parental authority in a manner that best meets the educative needs of children. Most nations already have laws designed to meet the needs of recomposed families, which includes those led by homosexuals.

Individuals desire to have children does not establish the right to have children (Bernheim, 2013). Presently, conditions for infertile heterosexual couples as it pertains to adopting are only granted if the circumstances are found to be more than adequate by a judge. If homosexual couples were permitted to adopt children, infertile heterosexual couples who are denied adopted children could correctly claim that they are the victims of discrimination. Clearly, homosexual couples are suffering because of their infertility, but no one has the right to be alleviated of their suffering at others expense. Therefore, homosexual couples' suffering is not a sufficient reason to permit homosexual adoption. For all adoption, it must be remembered that the rights of children are fundamental, and the right to children is secondary. Fundamental rights of children include giving adopted children to families that they will have the best chance at life. It is often believed that homosexual couples could assist in alleviating overcrowded adoption centers and help society by caring for children that would otherwise be stuck in orphanages, but it is the children that are in orphanages that need a father and mother more than other children to fill the basic emotional gap that has been given to him or her in life. This emotional gap can only be filled by a father and mother. Also, it is common for adopted children to reject one of the sexes of his or her adopted parents in order to reconcile emotionally with the loss of their biological parents. Homosexual adoption could potentially aggravate abandoned children through adoption, and logical individuals on both sides of the argument would agree that society does not have the right to risk the emotional wellbeing of children who have already been wounded. A society's legal system has an ethical obligation to ensure that a child's interests come first, and individuals must remember that every child has a right to a family. The intention of adoption is to address children's hardships and not to satisfy a couple's needs.

Although homosexual couples have the ability to have non-adopted children through medically assisted procreation, the inability to respect biological prohibitions on procreation does not offer sufficient ground to create legal realities for new forms of possible parenting (Bernheim, 2013). Homosexual activists have legally sought to lift limits on the rights of parenting because they are perceived as injustices and violations of the principles of equality, but the reality is that homosexual activists have used the principle of equality to seek medically assisted procreation to leverage their cause. New forms of homosexual parenting have created a vast array of possible combinations, and it is clear that these invented combinations are a result of attempting to legitimize homosexual parenting and to create universal rights for any possible combinations. It is clear that the array of possible parenting scenarios through medically assisted procreation and surrogate pregnancy goes far beyond the issue of homosexual parenting, so it is essential that the subject continued to be legally treated under the framework of legislation dealing with bioethics.

Many homosexual activists have sought to deny sexual differences through gender theory, which was first used by feminists in Western societies in the 1960s to denounce social differences that existed between males and females (Bernheim, 2013). The argument behind gender theory is that gender is attributable to norms and standards of societies' determination of what is masculine and feminine. Feminists interpreted these gender norms as the systematic basis for the domination of men over women within societies, and gender according to this interpretation is not based on biological sexual differences between males and females but on the social dimensions of sexual differences. Gender theorists support the notion that individuals are born without sex, and it is society that imposes gender-specific characteristics on individuals according to their biological sex. Gender theorists do not define individuals by their biological sex but by their sexuality, and there is an underlying tendency by these individuals to eliminate the biological and anatomical dimensions that separate the sexes. Gender theorists assume that sexual differences are an enduring cause of the subjugation between the sexes, and equality under this view results in the end of privileges based on sex within society because gender is viewed as purely a social construction and not as a natural category.

Queer theory takes gender theory to its extreme and seeks to return society to a stage of existence prior to sexual differences imposed on individuals prior to the current normative heterosexual sexual orientation (Bernheim, 2013). It seeks to remove all gender perceptions within society and language, which would in no way determine the psychic constitution of individuals because gender is reduced to a social construction. Since queer theorists remove the notion of sexual identity, individuals sexual orientations are based on the interior of their beings, so individuals can experience all forms of sexual desires independent of their biological sex. Under this theory, individuals masculinity or femininity become simple roles that they can choose to take on or reject, which essentially replaces individuals sexual identities with individual expressions that are unendingly created and recreated from relationship to relationship. Queer theorists demand social recognition for all forms of sexual orientations, and it is a fight that is clearly aimed at current social models of families and social conditioning that exists within societies. Acceptance of this view and the subsequent tolerance that would follow requires medical and legal institutions to adapt themselves to all forms of personal expressions of sexuality. It would be pointless under this view to deny homosexual marriage and adoption because it is the will of individuals that determines sex and not nature. In consideration of gender theory and queer theory, society is justified in questioning whether homosexual activists' purpose in seeking the legalization of homosexual marriage and adoption is the destruction of the foundations of society in an attempt to do away with ancestral morality and the very notion of sexual differences or not.

From a religious perspective, the complementary relationship between a man and a woman is fundamental, and theological accounts of the creation are grounded in sexual differences, which have functioned to support the duality of the sexes as part of the anthropological social code of humanity (Bernheim, 2013). All individuals are brought to the realization that they possess one of the two fundamental versions of humanity, and the other version will remain inaccessible and act to mark the finitude of themselves as individuals. A sexed being does not represent the totality of a species, and the theological definition of human being is only perceptible through a conjunction of both sexes. Sexual differences are not accidental acts of nature, and individuals genitals are physical expressions of sexuality that affect people's entire beings. The other sex will always remain unknowable to individuals who are male or female, and this puts sexual differences at the heart of nature and the limitations of individuals' self-sufficiency of being a gendered human being, which allows for the discovery of love that grows from a desire in the face of difference.

The underlying problem of proposed laws and enacted legislation that permit homosexual marriage and adoption is that they potentially harm the foundations of society as a whole for the benefit of a small minority (Bernheim, 2013). The problem with this type of legislation is that it disorganizes genealogies, children's statuses, and natural sexual identities. Life is a gift, and life has functioned according to given structures, order, and statuses prior to the powers of technology and imagination. Modernity has its full place within society but not at the expense of human and familial ecology, and children should be welcomed into societies to find their places without becoming objects and pawns in a power struggle.

Chapter 14: Children of Homosexuals

It is believed by many that homosexual behavior is replicable, specifically by youth who are influenced by their elders (Cameron, 2006). It is also commonly believed as a result of children mimicking of adults' behavior that environments with homosexual or gender-disturbed parents will be more likely to produce children that are homosexual or gender-disturbed. Research frequently cited by homosexual activists from the 1970s reported that children of homosexuals and transsexuals were not more likely to be homosexual or gender-disturbed than children of heterosexuals, and organizations like the American Psychological Association and the National Association of Social Workers has contended for the last four decades that the sexual interests of parents have minimal influences on the sexual desires of their children. If homosexual and other non-heterosexual desires exist randomly throughout populations, then common beliefs regarding the influence of homosexual and gender-disturbed behavior is wrong, and those concerned about allowing homosexuals to adopt children because of children's behavior emulation leading to homosexuality would be incorrect.

Research that has been done on children of homosexuals and transsexuals has focused on young children, and research focusing on the sexually active adult children is relatively unexplored (Cameron, 2006). As a result, controversy surrounding whether or not homosexual and transsexual parents are more likely to have homosexual and gender-disturbed children has continued. Research that has been done on young children's impersonation of homosexual behavior remains inconclusive to date, and researchers remain divided on the issue with some finding that there is no correlation and others arguing that current data sets are inconclusive. The reality is that the number of adult children of both homosexual and transsexuals researched has been modest at best. One of the underlying problems with researching homosexuals and transsexuals adult children is that there are fears among these parents. They believe that if children's sexual orientations are not found to be independent of their parents then this will influence social policies and will likely result in further barring homosexuals and transsexuals from becoming foster parents. There is a great deal of pressure among these parents to produce straight children, so parents that agree to participate in research often mysteriously disappear over time. This phenomenon has also been cited by journalists who were attempting to do profiles on homosexual and transsexual parents within families. The fear in the homosexual and transsexual communities about producing straight children has resulted in bias in research studies, and it opens up the possibility that there is underreporting by homosexual and transsexual parents regarding their children's adopted sexual inclinations.

Interviews that have been done with adult children with either homosexual or transsexual parents have revealed that there is intense pressure to appear to be heterosexual and to only reveal one's actual sexual orientation within either the homosexual or transsexual community (Cameron, 2006). Other interviews have revealed that many adult children of homosexuals and transsexuals are angry toward their parents, which has also contributed to bias research. All children, however, have a tendency to accommodate their parents' desires, and it is clear that these children are immersed in gay culture from an early age. Interviews have shown a great number of adult children of homosexuals and transsexuals who have reported being repulsed by heterosexuality as a result of being unfamiliar with it. Other adult children with either homosexual or transsexual parents who are heterosexual reported difficulties with making healthy decisions regarding heterosexual relationships as a result of a lack of experience, and some also reported ending heterosexual relationships abruptly out of fear being rejected by their homosexual or transsexual parents. There is a tendency among both homosexuals' and transsexuals' children to be apologetic of their parents' alternative lifestyles.

The extent of homosexual and transsexual parents influence on their children's sexual orientation cannot be confidentially estimated from the majority of previous data sets obtained in research studies because the children are not obtained randomly in the majority of them, and it is impossible to measure the level of influence of alternative lifestyle that each child has experienced (Cameron, 2006). In most of the research studies conducted to date, the children of homosexuals and transsexuals were born into heterosexual families, and then as one or more parent chose an alternative lifestyle children became increasingly exposed to homosexual and transsexual realities. In the one random sample that has been conducted of adult children with either homosexual or transsexual parents, 47% were homosexual or experienced homosexual desires. In non-random samples, 55% of adult children with either homosexual or transsexual parents were either homosexual or experienced homosexual desires. From the research that has been done on the influence of homosexual and transsexual parents on their children's sexual orientation, it can be definitively stated 47-55% adopt the sexual orientations of their parents, which is comparable to the influences of religion or smoking on children from heterosexual parents. There is a large correlation between parents and children's desires, but it is clear that more research must be conducted in this area that includes larger random samples, especially for

transsexual parents and their children.

Chapter 15: Attitudes toward Homosexuality

Over the last three decades, social science researchers have investigated attitudes toward homosexuality with a variety of approaches, and the results have shown that there is a substantial difference between individuals in their feelings toward homosexuality in accordance with their gender and race (Guittar & Pals, 2014). Gendered behavior is not a result of our genetic makeup but is a social construct, and gender socialization has created many cultural differences throughout the world in the manner in which men and women live their lives. Research from the early 1980s to the present has shown that men consistently hold more negative attitudes toward homosexuality than women, so gender has become one of the most explanatory determinants of attitudes toward homosexuality. In more recent decades, researchers have started to investigate racial differences and attitudes toward homosexuality, but the findings have been less consistent than those investigating attitudes toward homosexuality and gender. The majority of studies on attitudes toward homosexuality and race have concluded that Blacks have more negative attitudes toward homosexuals than Whites or Hispanics. In studies that have controlled for race, men have held greater negative attitudes towards homosexuals than women.

It is believed by researchers that the increased negative attitudes of Black men toward homosexuality is a result of concepts of masculinity and gender roles within their culture, which encourages social distancing from homosexuals within their own communities (Guittar & Pals, 2014). Some theorists have also put forth the idea that as a result of the oppression of White patriarchal society Black men rely more on heterosexual privilege, so it has resulted in increasing homophobia within Black communities. Other theorists have suggested that dominant White ideologies feminize Black males, and this has resulted in encouraging hypermasculinity among the Black males, which has increased Black men's negative attitudes toward homosexual behavior. Black men's anti-homosexual attitudes are believed by these theorists to be less about homosexuality and more of a flight from feminization imposed upon them through social constructs. Religiosity has been of particular interest to researchers because it is considered significant indicator of individuals attitudes toward homosexuality, and researchers believe that attitudes thought to be a result of race may actually be influenced by religiosity.

In countries where there is an emphasis on strong self-expression, religious beliefs have been important in explaining individuals' attitudes toward homosexuality (Guittar & Pals, 2014). Black men's religious beliefs were shown to be a statistically significant factor in their negative attitudes toward homosexuals among an all-Black sample of participants in one of the few studies considering gender differences and the effects of religiosity. Despite men's ethnicities, religious beliefs have been shown to yield greater negative influences on men's attitudes toward homosexuality than women, and this is believed by researchers to result from women being more compassionate and expressing an increased concern in general for the well-being of others despite being more religious than men. The effects of individuals' religious affiliations have also shown to vary in accordance with their attitudes toward homosexuality, and those with conservative religious associations are more influenced by religiosity in their attitudes toward homosexuality than those following more moderate ideological stances.

Attitudes toward homosexuality differ according to sex because of social constructions of gender, and individuals have different experiences associated to homophobia as a result of these differing constructions of gender (Guittar & Pals, 2014). Heterosexual men have a tendency to place a heavier emphasis on gender roles within society. In most societies throughout the world, men and women occupy different social positions: men are represented more in leadership roles, men earn higher salaries, men pay less for goods and services, men perform less domestic labor, and men are less likely to have their bodies scrutinized publicly. Gender role theory presumes that men and women have a tendency to display social behavior that is consistent with their sex, and the social roles for men in conjunction with their gender role beliefs has changed only minimally in comparison to women despite gender roles being contracted over time. Therefore, the consistency between traditional gender roles and women's actual behavior within society is less than that of men. Gender role beliefs have been shown to be the strongest predictors in attitudes toward homosexuality. Typically, individuals with strong gender role beliefs display the most negative attitudes toward homosexuality, and it is believed that this is a result of the strong threat that homosexuality presents to traditional gender role belief systems.

The combined effects of individuals' gender and ethnicity have not been shown to be significant predictors in people's attitudes toward homosexuality (Guittar & Pals, 2014). The combined effects of individuals' gender and religiosity have been shown to vary by gender, and women's attitudes toward homosexuality are not significantly influenced by their religiousness. Most gender differences in attitudes toward homosexuality can be explained by individuals' gender role beliefs and their level of understanding toward marginalized groups within society.

Individuals' concept of social justice is an important contribution toward their understanding of processes involving social change, and national attitudes toward homosexuality have been shown to be closely related to the legal protection for same-sex couples that are in place within countries.

Discussion

Many things have improved for homosexuals within Western societies over the last five decades, and it is clear that they will continue to do so into the future as the Gay Rights Movement maintains its fight for same-sex freedoms. Homosexuals are as diverse as any segment of the population, but their shared experience of victimization and discrimination will most likely continue to unite them well into the future (State Government of Victoria, 2014). It is clear that homosexuals in Western countries in which their rights have become legally protected still experience harassment and violence at points in their lives. This is especially true for young adults who report rates of verbal abuse at 60% and physical assault at nearly 20% as a result of their homosexuality. The continued victimization and discrimination of homosexuals within Western societies has resulted in increased mental disorders, higher rates of obesity, and increased alcohol and drug use in comparison to heterosexual members of society.

Most individuals base arguments against same-sex orientation and behaviors on religion, and they are correct in doing so. Abrahamic religions oppose homosexuality because the behavior is a sin and morally wrong according to theological interpretations. Western societies, however, are secular, so religion has no place in contemporary legal decisions despite it acting historically as a guide for societies throughout the world for millennia. Theological texts are open to interpretation, but religious scholars from Abrahamic religions have interpreted theological texts as being opposed to homosexuality throughout history. Religious institutions should accept homosexuals as individuals and respect their individual rights as members of societies, but they

138

should not be accepted as members of religious communities nor should homosexuals be accepted because they are practicing abstinence. It is okay to be homosexual, but it is immoral according to Abrahamic religions theological text interpretations and teachings.

For evolutionists, homosexuality has been paradoxical, but it is clear that in certain circumstances it can be an advantage and contribute indirectly to the distribution of ancestors through reciprocal altruism. Although homosexuality is not as frequent in nature as some gay rights activists would have the public believe, same-sex behavior has been recorded in nonhuman primates to maintain alliances. Homosexual behavior has been common throughout human history, especially as a result of certain environmental circumstances. There has been a great deal of research done on genetic and hormonal influence to homosexuality, and it is clear that there is an inherited and a prenatal hormone exposure component to same-sex preference. The scientific understanding of the genetic and hormonal influence on homosexuality is limited and not fully understood. There is a broad range of influences that contribute to homosexual behavior, so it is presently a mistake to categorize individuals on the basis limited scientific understanding regarding its influences.

Although homosexuality has existed nearly as long as heterosexuality as one of the broad ranges of behavior practiced by our ancestors, anthropologists have hypothesized that it was relatively rare, so it is considered evolutionary novel. It is believed that more intelligent people engaged in homosexual behaviors because the initial act of homosexuality would be considered a domain-specific adaptation to solving a problem. Since homosexuality is considered to be evolutionarily novel, the likelihood of intelligent people being homosexual increases, and more intelligent individuals are more likely to portray themselves as being homosexual because it is advantageous. Homosexual identities and behaviors are evolutionary novel because more intelligent children grow up to have same-sex preferences, and more intelligent people have more same-sex partners over the course of their lifetimes.

Homosexuality has become a medical exception by breaking the contemporary trend of medicalizing human problems, and the behavior has been nearly completely demedicalized in the twenty-first century. There are areas looming in genetic and psychological research that could potentially result in homosexuality being remedicalized, but it is clear that the gay community has been resilient in its lobbying to get homosexuality removed from the "Diagnostic Statistical Manual of Mental Disorders" and to overcome the social setbacks as a result of the HIV/AIDS epidemic. The shift in research over the last three decades has resulted in the scientific community looking for a genetic connection to homosexuality, and it is likely that slight genetic differences will be continued to be found between heterosexuals and homosexuals. Concerns that homosexuality could be considered a biomedical disorder in the future are real, but the gay community has used genetic research that has been performed to date to increase its rights. If the gay community continues to use genetic research in its favor, the likelihood of homosexuality being remedicalized as a result of inheritance is miniscule.

Homosexual communities have created their own norms and standards that have resulted in the development of a unique set of criteria being set around appearance and body image. These standards differ between homosexual men and women, and it is clear that psychologists working with these individuals must be aware of the pressure within these communities to overcome heteronormative oppression through sets of characterized norms created within homosexual societies, which will continued to be increasingly portrayed to these individuals through gay media and gay-specific advertising. Pressures to conform within homosexual communities regarding image has resulted in segregation within the community and has put same-sex oriented individuals at an increased risk for body image dissatisfaction disorders, especially homosexual men. As advertising increases that targets homosexual individuals, it is likely that rates of body image dissatisfaction will result in higher rates of low self-esteem, depression, and other disorders within the gay community. Although homosexual women have reported lower rates of body dissatisfaction than both heterosexual women and homosexual men, there has been limited research done in this area, but it is clear from the research that has been done to date that female homosexual relationships promote and increase satisfaction and acceptance of one's body image in comparison to heterosexual and male homosexual relationships.

Matrimony throughout history has historically embraced the concept man and woman partnering together, and it has functioned as a socially guiding principle to create generations through progeny. Individuals opposed to homosexual marriage cite acceptable rules that have functioned to guide nations throughout the world historically, and they view the acceptance of same-sex marriage as challenge the foundations of society. Those opposed to homosexual marriage believe that its acceptance could potentially lead to the destruction of society because it places the institution of marriage into a legal category that is sexless. Despite many individuals being opposed to both gay marriage and adoption as a result of religious interpretation, they are correct in their analysis regarding rights. Because a couple desires to be married or to adopt a child, it does not automatically give them the right to do so. Restrictions regarding legally permissible marriages still exist on individuals who are related and individuals seeking to marry multiple partners at the same time. Homosexual marriage should be endorsed by society in consideration of the psychological benefits that it offers same-sex couples and the health benefits of being in a lifelong relationship offers to individuals who are in communities that are at increased risk to HIV/AIDS exposure.

Homosexuality is a sin, and endorsement of homosexual unions by Abrahamic religious institutions contradicts its theological texts and religious teachings. Therefore, homosexual marriage should be permitted and legally sanctioned in societies with secular governments, but it should not be blessed by religious institutions because it contradicts the essence of their theological texts and teachings. Homosexual adoption is currently being permitted by law in the majority of states within the US despite homosexual adoption potentially harming the foundations of society to benefit a small minority. Legislation permitting same-sex couples to adopt has potentially disorganized genealogies, the status of children, and natural sexual identities. The social ramifications of same-sex adoption on the adopted children and society as a whole are presently unclear, and it is an area that needs to be closely monitored and researched for decades to come because of the potential for these adopted children to become pawns in a power struggle to increase the acceptance of homosexuals within society.

There have not been an adequate number of research studies done on the influence of homosexual parents on the children's sexual orientation. It is difficult to estimate the effects of alternative lifestyles of parents on children because it is nearly impossible to measure the level of influence on an individual basis that is experienced by children. Of the research that has been conducted through random sampling, it is clear that more than 50% of the children of same-sex couples adopt the sexual orientation of their parents. There is a large correlation between parents and children's sexual desires, but it is unclear if these effects will also be found for adopted children, especially in consideration of the fact that they do not share the same genes. The percentage of American men and women who are homosexual is roughly 25%, so it is clear the number of children inclined to have a same-sex orientation as a result of homosexual parental influence is higher than the rates of homosexuals found in the general population (Gallup, 2002). Actual rates of homosexuality among children of homosexuals and the general population may never be known because many homosexuals have trouble admitting their sexuality to themselves.

Attitudes toward homosexuality can be explained by individuals' gender role beliefs, and their level of empathy towards marginalized members of society. Despite women being more religious than men, their increased acceptance of homosexuality is clearly a result of their ability to show compassion and better concept social justice than men. Attitudes toward homosexuality are result of social constructions toward gender, which are shaped as a result of differing individual experiences. Heterosexual men place an increased emphasis on gender roles within most societies, and it is clear that heterosexual men will increasingly experience difficulty with the acceptance of non-traditional relationships within society because social roles have changed little for them over time. Heterosexual men have traditionally held the most consistent gender roles within society, and they have changed less than women. Homosexuality presents a threat to the gender role belief system of most heterosexual men, which can often be displayed in negative attitudes toward homosexuals. Increasing acceptance of homosexuals has resulted from legal progress made by the Gay Rights Movement in Western countries, and it will continue to do so as human rights violations that expose the permit the victimization and death sentences of homosexual individuals become increasingly exposed. Homosexuals have a place within all societies, and they have a right to sexual freedom that is free from victimization and discrimination. Despite homosexuality presenting a threat to heterosexual belief systems, homosexuality should be respected and protected within modern secular societies.

Reference Citations

Adoptive Families Magazine (2014). Adoptions by Same-Sex Couples Still on the Rise. Retrieved online from: http://www.adoptivefamilies.com/articles.php?aid=2321/.

Asal, V., Sommer, U., and Harwood, P. (2013). A Cross-National Study of the Legality of Homosexual Acts, *Comparative Political Studies*, 46(3), p. 320-351.

Bailey, N. & Zuk, M. (2009). Same-sex sexual behavior and evolution, *Trends in Ecology and Evolution*, 24(9), p. 439-446.

Balsam, K., Rothblum, E. and Beauchaine, T. (2005). Victimization Over the Life Span: A Comparison of Lesbian, *Gay, Bisexual, and Heterosexual Siblings*. Retrieved online from: http://tpb.psy.ohio-state.edu/papers/Balsam%20JCCP%202005.pdf

Bawkin, H. & Bawkin, R. (1953). Homosexual Behavior in Children, *The Journal of Pediatrics*, 43(1), p. 108.

Beredjick, C. (2012). DSM-V to Rename Gender Identity Disorder 'Gender Dysphoria'. Retrieved online from: http://www.advocate.com/politics/transgender/2012/07/23/dsm-replaces-gender-identity-disorder-gender-dysphoria

Bernheim, G. (2013). Homosexual Marriage, Parenting, and Adoption, *First Things*, 23(1), p. 41-50.

Bogaert, A. (2006). Study finds homosexuality more nature than nurture, *Kamloops Daily News*, 1(1), p. 1.

Cameron, P. (2006). Children of homosexuals and transsexuals are more apt to be homosexual, *Journal of Biosocial Science*, 40(3), p. 412-419.

Conrad, P. & Angell, A. (2004). Homosexuality and remedicalization, *Society*, 41(5), p. 32-39.

Friedman, R. & Downey, J. (1994). Special article: Homosexuality, *The New England Journal of Medicine*, 331(14), p. 923-930.

Gallup (2002). What Percentage of the Population Is Gay? Retrieved online from: http://www.gallup.com/poll/6961/what-percentage-population-gay.aspx.

Glaser, D. (2006). Are homosexual men more body conscious? The effects of media images on homosexual men's body image as compared to heterosexual men. The Chicago School of Professional Psychology, Illinois.

Grant, S. (1999). Can Animals Be Gay? New Books Stirs Debate Author Insists Homosexual Behaivor is Common in the Wild, *Hartford Courant*, p. 1.

Guittar, N. & Pals, H. (2014). Intersecting gender with race and religiosity: Do unique social categories explain attitudes toward homosexuality?, *Current Sociology*, 65(1), p. 41-65.

Friedman, M., Marshal, M., Stall, R., Cheong, J., and Wright, E. (2008). Gay-related Development, Early Abuse and Adult Health Outcomes Among Gay Males, *AIDS and Behavior*, 12(6), p. 891-902.

Harris, C. (2003). Homosexual Behavior in Children, *The Journal of Pediatrics*, 143(1), p. 80.

Herzog, D., Newman, K., Yeh, C., and Warshaw, M. (1992). Body Image Satisfaction in Homosexual Women and Heterosexual Women, *International Journal of Eating Disorders*, 11(5), p. 391-396.

homosexuality. (2014). In *Encyclopedia Britannica*. Retrieved from http://www.britannica.com/EBchecked/topic/270637/homosexuality

Jannini, E., Blanchard, R., Comperio-Ciani, A., and Bancroft, J. (2010). Male homosexuality: nature or culture?, *The Journal of Sexual Medicine*, 7(10), p. 3245-3253.

Kanazawa, S. (2012). Intelligence and Homosexuality, *Journal of Biosocial Science*, 44(5), P. 595-623.

Kirkpatrick, R. (2000). The Evolution of Human Homosexual Behavior, *Current Anthropology*, 41(3), p. 385-412.

Kortner, U. (2008). Sexuality and partnership: Aspects of theological ethics in the field of marriage, unmarried, and homosexual couples. Retrieved online from: http://www.google.com/url?sa=t&rct=j&q=&esrc=s&source=web&cd=1&ved=0CBwQF jAA&url=http%3A%2F%2Fwww.ajol.info%2Findex.php%2Fhts%2Farticle%2Fdownloa d%2F41282%2F8662&ei=caelU9ieC8y6kQXL54G4Cw&usg=AFQjCNGDPMHSyseT9 kVXwvXDHVYfr7hS6w&bvm=bv.69411363,d.dGI.

Lester, A. & Hayes, A. (2005). Homosexual Equality in the United Kingdom, *Peace Review*, 17(2), p. 149-154.

Levesque, M. & Vichesky, D. (2006). Raising the bar on the body beautiful: An analysis of the body image concerns of homosexual men, *Body Image*, 3(1), p. 45-55.

McBrayer, J. (2012). Christianity, Homosexual Behavior, and Sexism, *Think*, 11(31), p. 47.

New England Newspapers, Inc. (2013). Nurture vs. Nature, *The Brattleboro Reformer*, 1(1), p. 1.

NewsRx (2005). Perception; Potential pheromone activates brains of homosexual men, *Science Letter*, 1(1), p. 1431.

Savic, I., Berglund, H., and Lindstrom, P. (2005). Brain Response to Putative Hormones in Homosexual Men, *Proceedings of the National Academy of Sciences of the United States of America*, 102(20), p. 7356-7361.

Schmid, R. (2006). Study finds lesbians react to hormones like straight men; Suggests physical basis for homosexuality, *The Record*, 1(1), p. 12.

State Government of Victoria (2014). Gay and Lesbian Discrimination. Retrieved online from: http://www.betterhealth.vic.gov.au/bhcv2/bhcarticles.nsf/pages/Gay_and_lesbian_issues_discrimination.

Ungerfeld, R., Lacuesta, L., Damian, J., and Giriboni, J. (2013). Does heterosexual experience matter for bucks' homosexual mating behavior?, *Journal of Veterinary Behavior: Clinical Applications and Research*, 8(7), p. 474-477.

Vittorio, G. & Robinson, P. (2000). Is there a "Homosexual Brain"?, *The Gay and Lesbian Review Worldwide*, 7(1), p. 12.

Wilson, I. (1999). The Emerging Gay Adolescent, *Clinical Child Psychology and Psychiatry*, 4(5), p. 551-565.

149

About the Author

Alan Philowitz was born and raised in Phoenix, Arizona. His education consists of a bachelor's degree in English from Arizona State University and a master's degree in Psychology from University of Phoenix. He has been teaching, investing, and consulting for the past 12 years throughout the world. He has been an author for over 15 years, and he has published both fiction and non-fiction works during this period.